Second Treatise On The Effects Of Borax And Boric Acid On The Human System

SECOND TREATISE

ON THE

EFFECTS OF
BORAX AND BORIC ACID
ON THE HUMAN SYSTEM.

(WITH TWO SUPPLEMENTS.)

BY

DR. OSCAR LIEBREICH,

O. Ö. PROFESSOR DER UNIVERSITÄT BERLIN UND GEHEIMER MEDIZINALRAT.

(TRANSLATED FROM THE GERMAN.)

London:

J. & A. CHURCHILL,

7, GREAT MARLBOROUGH STREET.

1902.

PRICE TWO SHILLINGS AND SIXPENCE.

1693. d

SECOND TREATISE

ON THE

EFFECTS OF

BORAX AND BORIC ACID

ON THE HUMAN SYSTEM.

(WITH TWO SUPPLEMENTS.)

BY

DR. OSCAR LIEBREICH,

O. Ö. PROFESSOR DER UNIVERSITÄT BERLIN UND GEHEIMER MEDIZINALRAT.

(TRANSLATED FROM THE GERMAN.)

———

London :

J. & A. CHURCHILL,

7, GREAT MARLBOROUGH STREET.

—

1902.

CONTENTS.

	Page
Absorption of nitrogen in food containing boron preparations	62
Absorption of nitrogen in the intestine more favourable immediately after food containing Borax	65
Administration of Borax and Boric Acid to patients	10
Albumen in the urine after taking Boric Acid	5
Albuminuria	6
Albuminuria disappearing in the course of treatment with Borax ...	18
Albumiuuria observed during the treatment of patients with Boric Acid	12
Alkaline fermentation of the urine with Boric Acid	21
Alleged cases of death caused by Boric Acid	87
Alleged chronic effect of Boric Acid	48
Alleged diarrhœa in infants through preserved milk	48
Alleged diarrhœtic effect of Borax and Boric Acid	69
Alleged difference between the supposed irritative effect of Borax and Boric Acid on the mucous membrane	44
Alleged digestive derangements	46
Alleged increased disiutegration of cells	46
Alleged poisoning by food containing Borax	1
Application of saltpetre compared with that of boron preparations ...	44
Aseptine	16
Assimilation of food ... ... ⋯	59
Assimilation of food containing Borax	50
Assimilation of food not diminished by boron preparations	67
Assimilation of food when taking Borax	62
Binswanger ... ... ⋯	47, 75
Binswanger's experiment on himself	49
Bitter almonds, Effect of, on fowls	8
Bladder, Innocuousness of irrigations of, with Boric Acid ·	10
Bladder irrigations by means of Boric Acid	21
Borax admissible in large doses for therapeutic experiments	10
Borax cannot be considered as an abortive	14
Borax completely disappears out of the system	67
Borax, Cumulative effects of, on human beings considered	14
Borax, Effect of, on the absorbing capacity of the intestine	66
Borax entirely innocuous as regards the functions of the kidneys ...	10
Borax in cases of obesity	86
Borax injections into rabbits	8
Borax-preserved foods for expeditions and soldiers	81
Borax and Boric Acid, Administration of, to patients	10
Borax and Boric Acid, Alleged diarrhœtic effect of	69

iv   CONTENTS.

	Page
Borax and Boric Acid even in very large doses used in food produce no diarrhœa...	81
Borax and Boric Acid, Internal application of, has never yet proved fatal	87
Borax and Boric Acid soothing preparations	5
Boric Acid, Alleged chronic effect of	48
Boric Acid applied in cases of infection of the bladder	21
Boric Acid, Continued use of, in urological practice	21
Boric Acid for alkaline fermentations of the urine	21
Boric Acid in cases of tuberculosis ... ·	81
Boric Acid is held to be the most harmless of all antiseptic drugs at our command	10
Boric Acid, Prolonged use of, not injurious	22
Boric Acid, Treatment of eczema with	23, 24
Boric Acid when absorbed in the blood circulates as borate of sodium ...	10
Boric reaction, Disappearance of, from the urine	14
Boron compounds in persons suffering from kidney disease	48
Boron compounds and saltpetre, Comparison between	49
Boron excreted from the system normally	68
Boron preparations are absolutely harmless to the mucous membrane ...	45
Boron preparations, Consideration of, for internal use	21
Boron preparations, Effect of, in affections of the kidney and bladder ...	18
Boron preparations, Elimination of, from the system	67
Boron preparations, Excretion of	14, 48
Boron preparations in some cases reduce diarrhœa	81
Brunton Sir Lauder, on albuminuria	6
Bubo Gummosus, Experiment with patient suffering from	29
Cases of death, Alleged, caused by Boric Acid	87
Cats, Uselessness of experiments on, only	4
Causes of temporary appearance of albumen in the urine	6
Chittenden	59
Claude Bernard	6
Comparison between saltpetre and Boron compounds	49
Comparison of Boric Acid with alcohol in excretion from urine	15
Consideration of Boron preparations for internal use	21
Consideration of report of the Kaiserliches Gesundheitsamt	58
Criticism of the technical argument upon which the Bundesrat founded the resolution in regard to injurious and deceptive ingredients in meat	43 - 54
Cumulative effects of Borax on human beings considered	14
Cutaneous eruptions	49
Cystitis, Internal application of Boric Acid for	10
Declaration of the German Federal Council	84
Departmental Committee's Report	58

CONTENTS.

v

	Page
Dermatitis after scabies, Experiment with patient suffering from ...	31 - 33
Description of the normal kidney of a rabbit	9
Diarrhœa	69
Diarrhœa in infants through preserved milk, Alleged	48
Diarrhœa; None produced by Borax and Boric Acid even in very large doses	81
Digestive derangements, Alleged	46
Dog fasting, Experiment on	82 - 83
Dog, Inconclusive experiment on a...	47
Early instances of the application of Borax as a food antiseptic... ...	44
Eczema, Experiments on patients suffering from	34-5, 38
Eczema; Treatment with Boric Acid	23
Effect of bitter almonds on fowls	8
Effect of Borax on the secretion of the kidneys in animals, Experiments on	7
Effect of Borax and Boric Acid communicated to animals subcutaneously	71 - 72
Effect of boron preparations in affections of the kidney and bladder ...	18
Effect of milk on kittens, with and without Borax and Boric Acid ...	1
Effect of saltpetre on the mucous membrane of the stomach of a dog ...	47
Effect of soda on the mucous membrane of the stomach of a dog ...	47
Effect on the mucous membrane	45
Effect on the secretion of the kidneys	4
Effects of Borax on the skin	18
Effects of Boric Acid on the absorbing capacity of the intestine... ...	66
Effects of common salt	69
Elimination of Boric Acid in a case of kidney disease	67
Elimination of boron preparations from the system	67
Examination of urine of patients treated with Boric Acid	11
Excretion of boron preparations	14, 48
Experiments on a dog fasting	82
Experiments on cats only, Uselessness of	4
Experiments on fowls	2 - 4
Experiments on metabolism with Borax, by Neumann	80
Experiments on the effect of Borax on the secretion of the kidneys in animals	7
Experiments with Boric Acid showing nitrogen in urine...	63 - 64
Experiments with Borax and Boric Acid on the stomach...	73
Fæces, Observation of, of patients taking Boric Acid	75 - 80
Fish preserved with Borax and Boric Acid not injurious to health ...	58
Food, Assimilation of	59
Food, Assimilation of, containing Borax	50, 62
Food containing Borax, Alleged poisoning by	1
Foods for expeditions and soldiers, Borax-preserved	81

vi   CONTENTS.

	Page
Forster	59, 62
Fowls, Experiments on	2 - 4
Fritzweiler	75
Gaucher	81
Gerhardt, C.	81, 86
German proclamation concerning injurious and deceptive ingredients in meat	48
Glandular swelling in submaxillary region, Experiment with person suffering from	28
Guyon	21
Hager	44
Halliburton	53
Handford	49
Heffter	62, 69
Inconclusive experiment on a dog	47
Infection of bladder, Boric Acid applied in cases of	21
Inflammation, Alleged, of the mouth and throat caused by Borax	45
Injections of Borax into rabbits	8
Injuries from solution of caustic soda, Experiment with patient suffering from	39 - 40
Injurious and deceptive ingredients in meat, German proclamation re	48
Innocuousness of Borax as regards the functions of the kidneys	10
Innocuousness of irrigations of the human bladder with Boric Acid	10
Internal application of Borax and Boric Acid had never yet proved fatal	87
Internal application of Boric Acid for cystitis	10
Intestinal wall, Alleged increased disintegration of the cells of	46
Intestine, Effects of Borax on the absorbing capacity of the	65
Intestine, Effects of Boric Acid on the absorbing capacity of the	66
Intravenous injections of Borax solution in rabbits	17-20
Irrigating the bladder by means of Boric Acid	21
Irrigation of the stomach	50
Irritation, Symptoms of, in the kidneys	7
Johnson	75
Kidney disease, Boron compounds in persons suffering from	48
Kidneys	86
Kidneys, Borax entirely innocuous as regards the functions of the	10
Kidneys, Effect on the secretion of the	4
Kidneys in animals, Effect of Borax on the secretion of the	7
Kidneys, No irritation of, occurs even after large doses of Borax	18
Kister	4, 5, 49, 69
Kister's experiments on human beings	16
Kittens, Effect on, of milk with and without Borax and Boric Acid	4

CONTENTS.

vii

	Page
Lebbin	51
Le Bon	69
Liebreich	46, 59
Loss of weight	84
Loss of weight after food containing Borax	51
Loss of weight attributed to the increased waste of fat in consequence of consumption of Boric Acid	85
MacNaughton 13, 14, 17	
Mattern	47, 69
Medical practice maintains that Borax and Boric Acid are soothing preparations	5
Metabolism, Delicacy of experiments on	52
Metabolism experiments	60 - 61
Metabolism, Experiments on, with Borax, by Neumann	80
Metabolism, Rubner's experiment on	51
Milk extract, Directions for the preparation of	44
Mucous membrane, Alleged difference between the supposed irritative effect of Borax and Boric Acid on	44
Mucous membrane, Effect on	45
Nausea, Instances of	14
Neumann, R. O. 46, 52, 62, 67, 80, 85	
Nitrate of potash not harmless	54
Nitrogen, Absorption of, in food containing boron preparations	62
Nitrogen, Absorption of, in the intestine more favourable after food containing Borax	65
Nitrogen in the urine...	65
No effect on the kidneys of patients treated with Boric Acid	11
No irritation of the kidneys occurs even after large doses of Borax ...	18
Observation of the fæces of patients taking Boric Acid	75 - 80
Overdoses of preservatives	15
Patients, Treatment of, with Borax and Boric Acid	10
Periodical appearance of albumen in the urine	6
Pityriasis Rosea, Experiment with patient suffering from	86 - 87
Poisoning, Alleged, by food containing Borax	1
Polli	75
Posner, Prof. Dr.	10, 22
Preservatives, Overdoses of	15
Prolonged use of Boric Acid not injurious	22
Rabbit, Description of a normal kidney of a	9
Rabbits, Experiments with Borax and Boric Acid on, through the stomach	73
Rabbits, Injections of Borax into	8
Rabbits, Intravenous injections of Borax solution into 17	20

viii CONTENTS.

	Page
Rabbits, Subcutaneous experiments with Borax and Boric Acid on ...	72
Report of the Departmental Committee	58
Robinson, M. K.	1
Rhagades of the lower lip, Experiment with patient suffering from ...	25
Rose, Dr.	45
Rosemann	52
Rosenheim	52
Rosenthal	75
Rost ... ... 51, 58, 62, 66, 67, 70, 71, 75, 81 - 82, 86
Rubner 51, 85
Rubner's experiments on metabolism	51
Saltpetre, Application of, compared with that of Boron preparations ...	44
Saltpetre, Effect of, on the mucous membrane of the stomach of a dog...	47
Saltpetre and Boron compounds, Comparison between	49
Senator on albuminuria	6
Sir Lauder Brunton on albuminuria	6
Skin, Effects of Borax on the	13
Soda, Effect of, on the mucous membrane of the stomach of a dog ...	47
Sonntag 68, 75
Spear	44
Subcutaneous experiments with Borax and Boric Acid on rabbits ...	72
Summing up of Dr. Rost's experiments and observations on human beings	84
Symptoms of irritation in the kidneys	7
Tuberculosis, Boric Acid in cases of	81
Tunnicliffe	52
Ulcera dura penis, Experiment with patient suffering from	27
Ulcus durum laminæ internæ præputii, Experiment with patient suffering from	30
Ulcus durum penis, Experiment with patient suffering from	26
Urine, Albumen in the, after taking Boric Acid	5
Urine, Disappearance of Boric reaction from	14
Urine examinations of patients treated with Boric Acid	11
Urine, Nitrogen in the	65
Urotropin	22
Uselessness of experiments on cats only	4
Vigier	75
Virchow 5, 58
Vomiting	82
Water-torture...	74
Weight, Loss of	84
Weight, Loss of after food containing Borax	51
Wildner	75

SECOND TREATISE

ON THE

EFFECTS OF BORAX AND BORIC ACID
ON THE HUMAN SYSTEM.

IN the treatise on the effects of Boric Acid and Borax[1] (Berlin, 1899; printed as a manuscript) it was proved that Borax is not a poisonous substance, as was formerly maintained. It was also shown that therapeutic notions which were held about Borax, especially since Pidoux' and Trousseau's statements, are incorrect, and that therefore a prominent place must be conceded to Borax as a medical preparation, as well as a food preservative. The correctness of the above supposition was proved by means of historical and literary studies, and especially by experimental examination. It was possible to prove that no harmful influence was noticeable on the digestive ferments, or the epithelium of the digestive tract, likewise on the ferments which are to be found in the body. Further, no cases had occurred in practice which could justify a warning against the internal application of Borax. It therefore appeared by no means necessary at that time to prove these facts afresh by experiments on human beings. Later experiences which could shake the validity of these views are not forthcoming. Nevertheless, erroneous or insufficient observations, which were likely to encourage prejudice, have been made public, and therefore require to be refuted.

Especial excitement was caused by the assertion that a general poisoning had been caused by Borax. The author of this alarming news is Dr. M. K. Robinson.[2] Although the case has seldom been referred to in German

Alleged poisoning food con Borax.

---

[1] "Effects of Borax and Boracic Acid." London, J. & A. Churchill, 1899, and "Vierteljahresschrift für gerichtliche Medizin," 3rd ser., Vol. 19, 1.

[2] "Public Health." Aug. 1899, Vol. XI., No. 11.

scientific papers, it began by leading to a misunderstanding in England and requires to be cleared up first.

> " Five of seven persons in a house were suddenly taken ill, " after eating blanc-mange which had been made of milk from the " day before, and to which not only the milkman, but also the cook, " had added Boric Acid. Nine fowls which had been fed with the " remains of the blanc-mange became ill, and five of them died."

In the following paragraph it can be shown that this single proof of the effect being fatal entirely falls to the ground :—

No description is given of the symptoms in the human beings, or in the fowls. But we will leave the symptoms of the human beings out of the question, and we must also set aside the cause of the fowls' illness, for the fowls were not dissected. The question should be put to Mr. ROBINSON whether he never observed that sudden illnesses have occurred after blanc-mange, ice, milk, and the like food, without Borax or any other preservatives having been used. It is well known that illness often occurs after food which has been kept in metal dishes ; but the first thing for an examining health officer to do would be to ask what blanc-mange is made of. According to the cookery-books of various nations, the ingredients are as follows : Milk or cream, sweet or bitter almonds, sugar, gelatine, vanilla, orange-peel, bay-leaves.

It is obvious, therefore, that there are things in blanc-mange which, as is well known, sometimes cause poisoning of themselves. For instance, vanilla may often do so ; moreover, it is possible that poisoning by prussic acid may have occurred through too many bitter almonds. It cannot be objected that the bitter taste would prevent the people from eating it. The taste can be so effectually concealed by bay-leaves, lemon-peel, and other flavouring, that the dishes taste quite good, so that one is not prevented from eating them. Milk, which was already spoiled before the admixture of Borax or Boric Acid, might also have caused such a poisoning, for Borax or Boric Acid, as is well known, cannot make food sound which is already spoiled. Mr. ROBINSON ignored all this. It is now, of course, impossible to decide which of these contingencies was the right one. But it is possible to refute Dr. ROBINSON's formidable assertions thoroughly by means of experiments on fowls. He ought, perhaps, to have conducted these experiments himself, and so have proved whether fowls die on being fed with blanc-mange in which Boric

Acid is contained, before publishing such an unfounded assertion. In order to clear up all doubts on this subject, the following experiments were made:—

Nine fowls were fed with grain and kept under observation for several days. One of the fowls showed signs of difficulty in breathing and was therefore not used for the experiment. The following experiment was made on the remaining eight fowls:— *(Fowls fed with blanc-mange containing Boric Acid)*

1st day.—A thick pulp was made of 1,000 grammes of milk, 6·5 grammes of Boric Acid, and 200 grammes of maize meal, answering to the blanc-mange, and the eight fowls fed with it.

2nd day.—The same food.

3rd day.—Half the quantity was given.

In three days rather more than 2·0 grammes of Boric Acid per fowl was administered without disturbance being found in their condition. Their appetite for corn was by no means diminished.

12th day.—At 1 o'clock seven of the above-mentioned fowls had received ten pills, each containing 0·05 gramme of Boric Acid = 0·5 gramme and again at 3 o'clock the same dose, so that each fowl had received altogether 1 gramme of Boric Acid.

The eighth fowl received 50 grammes of sweet almonds.[1]

13th day.—No symptoms of illness appeared.

16th day.—*The fowls continue to be perfectly well.*

Hence we may deduce with full evidence—

1. That neither blanc-mange prepared with milk containing Boric Acid, even in such large doses as 6·5 : 1,000, is poisonous, nor that Boric Acid itself in such large quantities as 1-2 grammes had a toxic effect on these fowls.

2. That the signs of poisoning observed by Mr. ROBINSON in this case cannot have been caused by Boric Acid.

---

[1] Later experiments have shown me that bitter almonds have a very powerful effect on fowls through the prussic acid which is formed. After consuming 2 gr. a fowl showed an inclination to lie down. After 3 gr. a powerful effect took place within 25 minutes. The fowl lay on its side motionless and with greatly slackened breathing. This condition lasted for three hours. After four hours the fowl was found sitting upright, its breathing deep, regular, and slow. From that time the fowl recovered completely.

3. That Mr. ROBINSON did not succeed in tracing the poisoning to its true source.

Kister's experiments on fowls.

KISTER[1] repeated these experiments on fowls, but found that they did not stand such large quantities of Boric Acid as I had observed, which may perhaps be accounted for by difference of race in the fowls, or most likely because he fed them the whole time with too much concentrated Boric Acid, *i.e.*, in the form of pills, while in my experiments the greater part of the Boric Acid was given in blanc-mange. Nevertheless, the above-mentioned author comes to the same conclusion. He gives his opinion thus :—

> " ROBINSON traces these phenomena to the consumption
> " of Boric Acid, and takes it as a direct proof of the pernicious
> " effects of Boric Acid. Against this view LIEBREICH rightly brings
> " forward the fact that the proof of the injuriousness of Boric Acid
> " in this case is not convincing, since blanc-mange contains in-
> " gredients such as vanilla, bitter almonds, etc., which, as is known,
> " may sometimes cause poisoning."

It has thus been shown that Dr. ROBINSON's incorrect conclusion has led to an unnecessary suspicion as to the effect of Boric Acid.

Uselessness of experiments on cats only.

Experiments on cats have also been frequently cited as a proof of the poisonous effects of Boric Acid and its salts. It must here be mentioned from a pharmaco-dynamic point of view that the conclusions arrived at as to the effect on cats is not of the least use for judging the effect of a substance on human beings. Kittens have died after being fed with cow's milk which had been mixed with Borax and Boric Acid. But the same thing also occurs when kittens are fed with cow's milk *only*; they die almost without exception in consequence of this diet. How perversely cats react may be seen by the effect on them of prussic acid, and above all of valerian root (*Radix valerianæ*).

Now let us consider the most weighty objection, that is, *the effect on the secretion of the kidneys*.

On the effect of Borax and Boric Acid on the kidneys.

In my first treatise I emphasized the fact that until now no harm to the kidney had been observed through the use of Boric Acid and Borax. The passage runs thus :—

> " Weak and diseased kidneys bear Borax and Boric Acid
> " particularly well; in fact, they form remedies of great value in

---

[1] Zeitschr. f. Hygiene u. Infektionskrankheiten, Vol. 37, 1901, No. 2, p. 229.

5

"kidney diseases, as VIRCHOW's own case[1] shows. Moreover, in
"the animal experiments there was no trace of any disturbance in
"the function of the kidney," etc.

And no irritation of the kidneys was ever observed in later experiments;
on the contrary, medical practice still successfully maintains that Borax and
Boric Acid are soothing preparations. It therefore necessarily attracted
attention when Dr. J. KISTER suddenly made a statement to the contrary,
which must be submitted to a strict examination, particularly as many
medical men have accepted this opinion as an established fact. Dr. J. KISTER
expresses himself in the following terms (1. c., p. 232):—

"After the result of the experiments, I cannot but be of the
"opinion that Boric Acid, even when not taken in immoderately
"large doses, may have an injurious effect on healthy adults, when
"continually used. I am justified in this conclusion by the
"discovery of albumen in the urine of two healthy persons, after
"they had taken Boric Acid several times," etc.

KISTER bases his opinion on experiments upon human beings,
which were conducted with 3 grammes of Boric Acid daily. The Boric
Acid was mixed with butter and spread on bread, which was eaten as a sand-
wich with roast meat or cheese. These experiments can be seen in Appendix
I. According to these, it is shown that of the three persons, Dr. L., P., and
S., after taking 3 grammes of Boric Acid daily from 7th November, 1900,
albumen was found on 16th and 17th November in the urine of two of them,
Dr. L. and P , and that this disappeared the next day after the Boric Acid
had been stopped.

First, it must be observed that 3 grammes of Boric Acid were taken
in a relatively small quantity of food, so that an unequal distribution of the
Boric Acid resulted. However, this point is not of decisive importance; the
chief point is the presence of albumen and the consequent deduction made by
Dr. J. KISTER of irritation in the kidneys. We will now study the cases
brought forward by the above-mentioned author:—1, Dr. L.; 2, P.; 3, S.

No description is given of the age, individuality or bodily structure of
the persons experimented upon, and that, above all, should have been done

---

[1] See "Effects of Borax and Boric Acid," p. 21: "Vierteljahresschrift für gerichtliche
Medizin, etc." 3rd ser., Vol. 19, 1.

6

On the periodical appearance of albumen in the urine.

if any possible irritation of the kidneys were to be clinically examined. For medical experience shows that the periodical appearance of albumen in the urine is by no means exceptional, and that in that case the albumen is not to be regarded as a pathological product. Those who are accustomed to examine the urine of many people frequently find that albumen appears one day or another, and disappears again later of its own accord. But, especially in the case of this excretion of albumen, there appears no phenomenon of irritation of the kidney, for this is characterized by morphotic formations. Also in this case neither red nor white blood corpuscles are found in the urine.

The temporary appearance of albumen may be caused by a slightly catarrhal condition of the urethral, vaginal, and vesical mucous membranes. Besides, there is a possibility of the presence of sperm, so that an examination under the microscope must in no case be omitted. It must also be considered that there is an *alimentary excretion of albumen*, which CLAUDE BERNARD even observed in his own case, after eating a considerable quantity of eggs.

Senator's and Sir Lauder Brunton's opinion on albuminuria.

This has been briefly discussed by SENATOR in his article on "Albuminuria," in LIEBREICH'S Encyclopedia. It is as follows :—

"Albuminuria, that is the only sort which comes into question "here, is the so-called true albuminuria (*a. vera renalis*) in which "the urine, coming from the kidneys into the urinary passage, "contains distinct traces of albumen ; it is a symptom of various "diseases, but may also appear, as the experiments of modern times "have shown, under circumstances which cannot be called patho- "logical but are within the limits of health. This is applicable "especially to the albuminuria of new-born infants and also to the "so-called ' physiological albuminuria,' which, without other disturb- "ances of the health and without any objectively traceable organic "affection, occurs temporarily and especially after muscular "exertions, heavy meals, cold baths, psychological excitement, and "such like. This kind of albuminuria does not require special "treatment, since it disappears either of itself, or when the above- "named causes are avoided."

These short and very clearly-put words express a universally accepted view, for other authors, such as Sir LAUDER BRUNTON[1], have expressed the same opinion as SENATOR.

[1] "On Disorders of Assimilation, Digestion, etc." London. 1901.

After the appearance of albumen in the urine in the cases of the two above-named individuals—Dr. L. and P.—the experiment was broken off, so that it is impossible to ascertain clearly whether in this case a *periodical excretion of albumen occurred, or whether the excretion of albumen can be connected with the consumption of Boric Acid.* To draw conclusions from KISTER'S experiments as to the connection between the consumption of Boric Acid and albumen in the urine must, therefore, be designated as inadmissible.

In the examination of substances capable of causing irritation of the kidneys, the pharmaco-dynamical rule holds good that, when at the beginning of its action a substance causes irritation of the kidneys, so that only albumen, without white and red blood corpuscles or other formed elements, is present in the urine, a severer irritation takes place if the substance continues to be taken, so that then red and white blood corpuscles, renal casts, and all the symptoms of an acute irritation of the kidneys are recognisable. For instance, in the case of Cantharides, we see that the first symptoms of irritation are announced by the presence of albumen, as can sometimes be observed after applying Spanish blistering plaster to the skin, as the cantharidine contained therein is absorbed through the skin ; but the most characteristic part is that then, if the application of Cantharides is continued, the excretion of albumen does not cease, red and white blood corpuscles are observed in the urine, and all the symptoms of irritation of the kidneys appear clinically, pathologically, and anatomically.

Since no irritation of the kidneys through the application of Boric Acid and its salts has until now been proved, it was urgently necessary to take up this question again ; but in consideration of the great responsibility resting on every author of therapeutic experiments, after KISTER's observations it appeared necessary to undertake some experiments on animals, in order to make sure whether an injurious effect on the kidneys may be discovered in sensitive animals after very large doses. It is just in this question of irritation of the kidneys that judiciously conducted preliminary experiments on animals are decisive for the formation of an opinion on the effect in the case of human beings. Though 'there are certain substances causing irritation of the kidneys in human beings, which are harmless to many animals, we know of no substances causing irritation of the kidneys in human beings which do not produce the same effect on rabbits, so that these animals may be used in properly conducted experiments as a proof for or against the acceptation of a toxic effect on the human kidneys. Experiments in feeding, it is true, are not alone determinative in this case, because the substances taken are unequally absorbed. For this reason intravenous injection is most suitable, so as to incorporate as large a quantity as possible in the rabbit's body. Unfortunately this method has the disadvantage that the injections cannot be continued over a long span of time, as the veins easily become obstructed ; but it is nevertheless possible, with great care, to continue the injections for some days without injuring the general health of the animals by this operation, and thus to arrive at a sufficiently accurate judgment. Therefore the experiments, the results of which are given in Appendices 2 and 3, shall be briefly described here.

The solution used for injection consisted of—Borax 10 grammes, common salt 1·56 grammes, and distilled water 170 ccm. As the Borax was apt to crystallise and separate from the solution on cooling, it was kept up to blood heat. Nine experiments sufficed to arrive at a result. All the experiments—also one which failed (as always occurs in experiments on animals)—shall be given for the sake of completeness.

The first animal received an injection of 6 cubic centimetres = 0·3528 gramme of Borax ; it died after $14\frac{1}{2}$ hours without any traceable cause of death.

The second animal received 6 cubic centimetres = 0·3528 gramme of Borax ; it remained in a normal state for 72 hours, and was then killed.

The third animal received 10 cubic centimetres = 0·588 gramme of Borax ; as the one vein proved to be obstructed, the injection was made into the other, after which the animal was killed.

The fourth animal received 10 cubic centimetres = 0·588 gramme of Borax, and as the canula was impassable, it was killed after 72 hours

The fifth animal was not used, as violent hæmorrhage occurred during the operation.

The sixth animal received 6 cubic centimetres = 0·3528 gramme of Borax and died in 24 hours, an affection of the lungs having become evident, such as often occurs in consequence of injections.

The seventh animal received an injection of 13 cubic centimetres = 0·7646 gramme of Borax ; as the vein became obstructed after 48 hours, the other vein of the neck was used, and the animal, which was otherwise sound, was killed after 72 hours.

The eighth animal received 14 injections, *i.e.* 0·8235 gramme of Borax, and was killed after 72 hours, being otherwise in a normal condition.

The ninth animal received 30 cubic centimetres = 1·764 grammes of Borax in 89 hours, during which time it was *perfectly normal*, and was then killed.

In the case of all the animals, with the exception of No. 5, which was not examined, the kidneys showed no abnormal condition. For the microscopic examination they were treated according to the method given in Appendix 3.

Now, let us here consider the normal kidney of the rabbit for the benefit of the uninitiated. For this a diagram and a photograph of the transverse section of a rabbit's kidney are necessary (Plate I.). We see at the margin *a* the corticle substance with the *glomeruli d* and the *tubuli contorti*, then the intermediary matter *a* , in which are HENLE's loops, towards the middle the *medulla renis b*, with its *tubuli recti c*. In the diagram we see further the pelvis of kidney *e*, the urethra *f*, and the vascular section *g*, as well as the fat on the hilus of the kidney *h*. Sections were made in every single portion of the kidneys of all the animals, and it proved impossible to discover any trace of a deviation from the normal condition. First we see by the *glomeruli* that the epithelia of the vascular loops and BAUMANN's *capsuli* are neither increased nor swollen. No pathological secretion is noticeable within the capsular cavity; the vascular loops themselves are of a normal shape and contain a normal quantity of blood. The cells in the *tubuli contorti* are normal in shape, and partly project dome-shaped into the *lumen*, partly show *striae*, a phenomenon which occurs when the cells do not secrete. At the basis of the cells the radiated streaks are distinctly visible in all cases. The nuclei are present in normal number and shape everywhere, the epithelia of HENLE's loops are likewise unchanged. The *tubuli recti*, which in themselves are capable of more resistance, show no change whatever. The interstitial tissue appears as usual and shows neither an increase of the connective tissue, nor an alteration of the blood vessels. Finally, no trace is present of an emigration of cells from the vessels either into the interstitial tissue or into the *tubuli uriniferi*, as is to be seen in Plates 2—5. Thus *not the faintest trace of a pathological change* occurs in consequence of this inundation with Boracic preparations. The illustrations showing sections of normal kidneys are in no way distinguishable

[margin note: Description of the normal kidney of a rabbit.]

in principle from those of the animals experimented upon (see the Appendices). The experiments with Boric Acid could be dispensed with, since Boric Acid, when absorbed in the blood, circulates as borate of sodium.

From these experiments on animals may be deduced that Borax is entirely innocuous as regards the functions of the kidneys.

It must be emphasized that few other substances exist, which could be intravenously imparted to a rabbit in such large quantities without injurious effect. Therefore these results make it admissible to use Borax in large doses for therapeutic experiments.

Innocuousness of irrigations of the human bladder with Boric Acid.

Besides hitherto existing clinical experience and these experiments on animals, a further support of the application of Borax to human beings was communicated to me by Professor Dr. POSNER, who has a wide experience through years of extensive practical activity. The report communicated to me will be found in detail in the fourth Appendix. I will merely emphasize the fact that thousands of irrigations of the bladder and even of the pelvis of the kidney have been performed by means of a catheter, without any poisonous effects being caused. Prof. POSNER says in this connection :—" In any case, " of all antiseptic drugs at our command, Boric Acid is held to be the most

Internal application of Boric Acid for cystitis.

" harmless." And in favour of internal application one case is especially instructive :—" A superior officer, whose position requires him to undergo " many bodily exertions, and in taking part in hunting, travelling, " and festivals, frequently to put up with a far from hygienic way of " living, has suffered from chronic-atonic cystitis for thirteen years. At " first he took Boric Acid constantly for some weeks, then, on becoming " better, left it off, but always had the remedy with him and took it again on " the slightest relapse. His general health remained excellent, and he never " observed the least unpleasant effect of this remedy, which he highly " valued. The doses were 0·5 gramme each."

Administration of Borax and Boric Acid to patients.

Therefore Boric Acid and Borax could be safely used in the case of various patients (Appendix 5, cases 1-12). In my practice seven patients were treated with Boric Acid and five with Borax, whilst the other necessary treatment was continued. In order to gain a correct clinical view of these patients, their life-history and the nature of their disease is given, and, according to my previous medical experience, I had to allow a continued use of Boracic preparations in the event of albumen appearing, in order to arrive at a decisive result. The choice was made between patients, who by their skin diseases showed a sensitiveness to affections of the skin, or who already had an infection of the skin, in order, at the same time, to observe the possible effect of Boracic preparations on the skin. The patients received finely powdered Borax and Boric Acid in a cup of milk; the part not dissolved was equally distributed before drinking by means of energetic stirring; after taking the beverage they received a biscuit or a roll. All the patients took this food without resistance.

The entire quantity of *Boric Acid* used in 93 *days* for 7 *patients* was 232·4 *grammes*.

Patient FRANZ F. received ... 4 days, per day 0·2 grm. = 0·8 grm. of Boric Acid
       7 ,, ,,   0·3 ,, = 2·1 grms. ,,
       1 day   1·0 grm. ,,
       12 days ,,   3·0 grms. = 36·0 grms. ,,

       In 24 days, total amount :   39·9 grms. of Boric Acid

Patient BERNHARD R. received 2 days, per day 0·2 grm. = 0·4 grm. of Boric Acid
       7 ,, ,,   0·3 ,, = 2·1 grms. ,,
       1 day   1·0 grm. ,,
       2 days ,,   2·0 grms = 4·0 grms. ,.
       10 ,, ,,   3·0 ,, =.30·0 ,,   ,,

       In 22 days, total amount :   37·5 grms. of Boric Acid

Patient GUSTAV W. received... 11 days, per day 3 grms. = 33 grms. of Boric Acid
Patient OTTO PR.   ,,   11 ,, ,, 3 ,, = 33 ,,   ,.
Patient JOHANNES K. ,,   11 ,, ,, 3 ,, = 33 ,,   ,,
Patient AUGUST F. ,,   7 ,, ,, 4 ,, = 28 ,,   ,,
Patient CHRISTIAN F. ,,   7 ,, ,, 4 ,, = 28 ,,   ,,

The urine of every patient, which was examined per day, showed no albumen, so that after these experiments with Boric Acid *no effect on the kidneys can be admitted*.

Borax was administered *to 5 patients*, 160·7 *grms.* in 123 *days*.

Female patient MARIE G. received... 1 day   . 0·2 grm. of Borax

4 days,	per day	0·3 grm.	= 1·2 grms.	,,
3 ,,	,,	0·4 ,,	= 1·2 ,,	,,
13 ,,	,,	0·5 ,,	= 6·5 ,,	,,
5 ,,	,,	1·0 ,,	= 5·0 ,,	,,

In 26 days, total amount :   14·1 grms. of Borax

Patient ALFRED L. received   ... 5 days, per day 0·3 grm. = 1·5 grms. of Borax

3 ,,	,,	0·4 ,,	= 1·2 ,,	,,
6 ,,	,,	0·5 ,,	= 3·0 ,,	,,
3 ,,	,,	1·0 ,,	= 3·0 ,,	,,
15 ,,	,,	2·0 grms.	= 30·0 ,,	,,

In 32 days, total amount :   38·7 grms. of Borax

Patient OTTO PA. received   ... 1 day   0·2 grm. of Borax

5 days,	per day 0·3 grm.	= 1·5 grms.	,,
3 ,,	,, 0·4 ,,	= 1·2 ,,	,,
8 ,,	,, 0·5 ,,	= 4·0 ,,	,,
2 ,,	,, 1·0 ,,	= 2·0 ,,	,,
2 ,,	,, 2·0 grms.	= 4·0 ,,	,,
16 ,,	,, 3·0 ,,	= 48·0 ,,	,,

In 37 days, total amount :   60·9 grms. of Borax

Female patient ELISE L. received ... 4 days, per day 1 grm. = 4 grms. of Borax

10 ,,	,,	2 grms.	= 20 ,,	,,

In 14 days, total amount :   24 grms. of Borax

Female patient LUISE M. received ... 5 days, per day 1 grm. = 5 grms. of Borax

9 ,,	,,	2 grms.	= 18 ,,	,,

In 14 days, total amount :   23 grms. of Borax

This series of experiments is of special interest, as albuminuria. was observed during the treatment, firstly in the case of the patient

Otto Pa., the same only lasting one day and disappearing in the course of the treatment with Borax ; secondly, in the case of the female patient Marie G., who on the eleventh day, after receiving a total amount of 3·6 grms. of Borax, passed urine, which on being boiled with nitric acid showed slight opalescence, but on the admixture of acetic acid and ferrocyanide of potash it gave no albuminous reaction. On the twelfth day, however, a decided turbidness was obvious, so that the presence of albumen could be considered as beyond doubt. The urine was consequently carefully examined, but was found to contain no urinary casts, or red or white blood corpuscles. Upon centrifugalising the urine, a not inconsiderable sediment was deposited ; it contained vesical epithelium. To obtain the pure urine the bladder was emptied by means of a catheter ; the urine was somewhat troubled and left a deposit on being centrifugalised, which showed upon examination only vesical epithelium and some few leucocytes, but no casts. Experience suggested continuing the application of Borax. On the thirteenth day the urine showed only a slight opalescence upon examination. *On the fourteenth day the albumen had entirely vanished, and even after the further application of 8·5 grammes, in fifteen days no more albumen appeared in the urine,* in connection with which it must be kept in mind that from the 14th to the 20th January 1 gramme of Borax was taken daily. The case was therefore evidently one of incipient catarrh of the bladder, which disappeared during the Borax treatment, and, as may be justly supposed from previous experience, in consequence of the Borax treatment. This case is of special interest, moreover, for this reason, that it proves the necessity of making long-continued observations, without which one is not in a position to maintain that a substance has had an irritating effect on the kidneys. This is also a further proof that Boron preparations have a beneficial effect in cases of affections of the kidney and bladder.

Thus it may also be considered as proved in the case of the use of Borax, that no irritation of the kidneys occurs even after large doses. The experiments made by Mr. MacNaughton on himself (see page 14) also proved that no albumen was excreted through the urine after the use of Borax and Boric Acid. It now remains to sum up the other experiences, gained from the treatment of these patients. _{Summing up of the results of the treatment.}

Firstly, it was shown that no harm in any direction resulted from the application of Borax to any patient. In the case of the skin no injuries occurred, as has been maintained to be the case after very large medicinal doses. In case No. 6, the patient suffered from *acne rosacea* in the nose, which increased during the application of Boric Acid ; but he had a cold in the head at the same time, so that the aggravation of this ailment, which often occurs of itself, cannot with any degree of certainty be attributed to the Boric Acid. In case No. 1, nausea and pains in the intestine occurred ; but the pains are evidently to be attributed to the aperients, as they completely disappeared eventually during the continued use of Boric Acid. Also the nausea, which the patient, Franz F., felt during an angina, cannot be attributed to the drug, as the nausea stopped during the continued application, when the angina disappeared. Likewise the nausea in case No. 8, the female patient, MARIE G., cannot be attributed to Borax, since she frequently experienced such phenomena during the period, and since, as I may remark, she was pregnant, which had been discovered later. By the way, this case has the further interest of showing that Borax cannot be considered as an abortive.

of para-

The objection has been raised, although no proof whatever has been given thereof, that Borax has a cumulative effect on human beings. It has been proved on animals, as is mentioned in my first treatise, that after the disappearance of the Borax in the urine, the various component parts of the animal's body contain no Boron combination. In a normal human being no Boron is to be found in the urine, under the strictest examination, after 8 to 12 days.

Although the results of a great number of experiments on the excretion of Boron preparations in the urine are on record, some new experiments were made. Mr. MacNaughton, a surgeon in Edinburgh, 44 years old, and in good health, made them on himself under my control.

1. On the 8th November, 1901, he took 3 grammes of Borax, which were washed down from the tongue with water. The urine was examined daily until the 19th November and contained Boric Acid ; on the 19th no more Boric Acid could be discovered by the flame-test in urine concentrated to $1/5$.

2. On the 22nd November, 1901, he took 3 grammes of Borax which were washed down from the tongue with water. The urine was examined daily until December 1st. In the afternoon of November 27th no more Boric Acid could be found in urine concentrated to $1/5$.

3. On December 2nd, 1901, he took 3 grammes of Borax, which were washed down from the tongue with water. The urine

was examined daily until December 11th ; on December 8th it was evaporated to 1/5 and showed no Boracic reaction.

The same gentleman took 0·5 gramme of Boric Acid with bread and butter on December 20th, 1901. The urine was examined until December 26th ; on that day the urine showed no Boracic reaction when concentrated to 1/5.

From these experiments it can be deduced that the Boracic reaction may disappear from the urine as early as the 5th and 6th days ; on the other hand, that an excretion was observed on the 11th day ; and it is not impossible, as other experiments have proved, that Boric Acid may be present in the urine some days longer. All the experiments upon which this work is based have been made with such large doses as are not requisite for the preservation of food. If, in certain cases, overdoses of preservatives have been proved by analysis, these are exceptions, caused by the fact that the manufacturers have not fixed their attention on the amount of the dose, because no injury has ever been observed, even after large doses.

The conclusions to be drawn from this, in connection with the experiments on animals, must not tend to the opinion that accumulation took place in the organism, but rather that, as is the case with many substances, a gradual excretion takes place. Let alcohol be cited here, in the case of which it was observed that after drinking a bottle of Moselle containing $10^o/_o$ of alcohol, the latter was found by means of fine reaction in the urine eight days later, although the bulk of the alcohol had become oxidized in the organism. So I think this frequently repeated objection to Boron preparations must be dropped.

The above-named investigations offer a further proof that Borax and Boric Acid are substances which cause no injury to health when judiciously used.

APPENDIX 1.

Kister's Experiments on Human Beings. Dose: 3 grms. of Boric Acid daily.

(The Boric Acid mixed with butter and spread on bread, which is eaten with meat or cheese.)

Date.	Dr. L.	P.	S.
7 Nov.1900.	Health good. Boric Acid in the urine after 2 hours, no albumen	——	——
8	Health good. Boric Acid in the urine, no albumen	——	——
9	Ditto	——	——
10	Ditto	——	——
11	Ditto	——	——
12	Ditto	——	——
13	Loss of appetite	——	——
14	Ditto	Health good; appetite normal; no albumen in the urine. Boric Acid in the urine	Diarrhœa, indisposition. Boric Acid in the urine, no albumen
15	Ditto	Ditto	Diarrhœa, nausea. Boric Acid in the urine; no albumen
16	Albumen in the urine	Ditto	——
17	Ditto	Albumen in the urine	——
18	Experiment broken off	Experiment broken off	——
19	No albumen in the urine	No albumen in the urine	——

APPENDIX 2.

Intravenous injections of Borax solution in Rabbits.

(Borax, 10 grms.; common salt, 1·56 grms.; water, 170 ccm.)

EXPERIMENT I.

27th Nov., 1901.—6 ccm. of Borax solution were injected into the left *vena jugularis communis* of a moderately strong rabbit in the course of 13 minutes. The animal became very weak and would take no food. Next morning at nine o'clock the animal was found dead, but still warm, and the kidneys were taken out for microscopic examination. The cause of death could not be discovered, but was probably an unrecognisable mistake in the operation on my part.

EXPERIMENT II.

29th Nov., 1901.—6 ccm. of Borax solution were injected into the left *vena jugularis communis* of a medium sized rabbit within 6½ minutes. The animal took food immediately after the operation.

30th Nov.—Took food and was lively.

1st Dec.—Ditto.

2nd Dec.—Ditto. Killed at 6.30, and the kidneys immediately removed for microscopic examination.

EXPERIMENT III.

30th Nov., 1901.—2 ccm. of Borax solution were injected into the *vena jugularis communis sinistra* of a moderately strong rabbit at 7 o'clock in the evening. Time of injection, 1 minute. The animal began to feed after half-an-hour.

1st Dec.—Health of animal normal.

2nd Dec.—7 p.m. Health normal, Injection of 2 ccm. of Borax solution.

3rd Dec.—The animal lively and feeding. An attempt to inject 2 ccm. more by means of the canula failed. The blood in the vein proved to be coagulated; an abscess had formed in its neighbourhood. Now 6 ccm. were injected into the *vena jugularis externa dextra* in the course of 6 minutes. The animal was rather weak, and sat motionless at first. About a quarter of an hour later the animal began to feed. At 7.35 it was killed and one kidney immediately laid in sublimate. The urinary bladder was removed by ligature at the vertex and taken out to get the urine. The urine, on examination with ferrocyanide of potash and acetic acid, showed traces of albumen.

EXPERIMENT IV.

9th Dec., 1901.—Moderately strong rabbit; urine free from albumen from 6th to 9th Dec. 6 ccm. of Borax solution were injected into the left *vena jugularis communis* on 9th December. Time of injection, seven minutes. Animal lively and feeding.

10th Dec.—Wound looking well. 2 ccm. of Borax solution injected.

11th Dec.—Urine contains no albumen. Injection of 2 ccm. of the solution.

12th Dec.—Urine contains no albumen. Coagulation in the vein. Killed. Slight suppuration in the neighbourhood of the vein. Urinary bladder considerably distended and filled with turbid urine. The turbidity disappears on the admixture of acetic acid. No albumen.

EXPERIMENT V.

Violent hæmorrhage occurred during the operation. The experiment was therefore discontinued.

EXPERIMENT VI.

13th Dec., 1901.—A rabbit received 6 ccm. of Borax solution at 10.25 *intravena*. Animal lively.

14th Dec.—Animal died in convulsions at 11 o'clock. Kidneys taken out fresh and laid in sublimate and formalin respectively. Urine free from albumen. Cause of death: *atelectasis pulmonum; thrombosis?*

EXPERIMENT VII.

14th Dec. 1901.—6 ccm. of Borax solution injected *intravena* into the *vena jugularis dextra*. Duration 6 minutes. Animal lively, feeding.

15th Dec.—4 ccm. injected at 5.30 p.m. No albumen.

16th Dec.—Thrombosis in the vein, injection impossible ; slight beginning of suppuration. Injection of 3 ccm. in *vena jugularis interna.*

17th Dec.—Killed. Bladder distended *ad maximum.* No albumen contained. Slight suppuration in the neighbourhood of the *vena jugularis communis sinistra.* Thrombosis here and in the *vena jugularis interna dextra.* Kidneys laid in sublimate and formalin respectively. Microscope reveals no peculiarity.

EXPERIMENT VIII.

14th Dec. 1901.—Rabbit, the same method of experiment as in VII. Duration of the injection 7 minutes. Animal lively, feeds immediately.

15th Dec.—5.30 p.m. 4 ccm. injected.

16th Dec.—Without albumen. 5.15 p.m. 4 ccm. injected.

17th Dec.—No albumen. Animal killed at 7 p.m. Thrombosis of the vein. Kidneys put in formalin and sublimate respectively. Microscope reveals no peculiarity.

EXPERIMENT IX.

1st Jan. 1902.—Black rabbit received 8 ccm. of the solution *intravena.* Wound treated with sublimate.

1st Jan.—Injection of 8 ccm. at 4.30 p.m.
2nd Jan.—Injection of 2 ccm. at 12 noon ⎫ Canula closed by means
2nd Jan.—Injection of 4 ccm. at 7 p.m. ⎬ of cotton wool saturated
3rd Jan.—Injection of 4 ccm. at 11 a.m. ⎭ with sublimate.
3rd Jan.—Injection of 4 ccm. at 8 p.m.
4th Jan.—Injection of 4 ccm. at 12 noon.
4th Jan.—Injection of 4 ccm. at 7 p.m.

The urine so far examined, was free from albumen.

5th Jan.—No albumen in the urine ; animal killed at 11.45 a.m. Nothing peculiar on dissection. Kidneys immediately put in sublimate.

The urine was free from albumen in all cases.

APPENDIX 3.

The kidneys were placed in a concentrated aqueous sublimate solution immediately after killing, and remained in this solution for 6 hours in the temperature of the room. Thereupon they were rinsed in running water for about 24 hours, put in gradually increasing percentages of alcohol up to absolute alcohol, in each for about 24 hours (80 °/$_o$, 90 °/$_o$, 100 °/$_o$), in 100 °/$_o$ they lay again for about 24 hours ; thereupon 24 hours in xylol, in a mixture of xylol and soft paraffin, then in soft paraffin. Then they were left in a mixture of 3 parts of hard paraffin and 1 part of soft for 24 hours, then poured out and cut.

The sections were put on to the object-glass with glycerine and albumen, and placed in the *incubator* at 52° C. for about 24 hours, then removed into oil of turpentine and alcohol, the concentration of which was gradually decreased. The last 70 °/$_o$ alcohol was mixed with tincture of iodine to remove the sublimate deposit, then the sections were placed in fresh 70 °/$_o$ alcohol to remove the iodine, until they were white. They were then put in water for some minutes, coloured with hæmatoxyline, laid in water for some hours and counter-coloured by means of alcoholic eosine, rectified with alcohol, cleared in *oleum origani* and embedded in Canada balsam.

APPENDIX 4.

BERLIN, *29th Dec.*, 1901.

DEAR SIR,

In answer to your esteemed communication concerning the application of Boric Acid in cases of diseases of the lower urinary passages, I beg to communicate the following facts :—

Boric Acid is in continual use in urological practice, being chiefly used externally for irrigating the bladder. For several years we have chiefly used concentrated Boric Acid solution (about 30 pro mille)[1] in water, partly as a remedy for slight cases of cystitis (especially for those caused by coli-infection), also partly in the preparatory irrigations, necessary for operations with the cystoscope. I may say that in the thousands of such irrigations performed by me personally, no symptoms pointing to poisoning have ever been observed, although there have frequently been cases of catarrhs of the bladder, deprived of the epithelium, in which an absorption is very possible. We do not shrink from irrigations of the renal pelvis with Boric Acid, neither has a case of poisoning come to my knowledge here. In any case, of all the antiseptic remedies at our disposal, Boric Acid is considered the most innocuous.

In the internal use of Boron preparations two questions have to be considered : it is used for purposes of " internal disinfection " and of alkalising the urine in cases of acidity. The latter purpose is served by administering Borax, although also pure Boric Acid appears in the urine in this form, so that its application would not be irrational. If it is stated that Boric Acid is a remedy for alkaline fermentation of the urine, Boric Acid fulfils this duty at most but indirectly, by destroying the causes of fermentation or stopping their development, but not by acting as a urophanous acid and influencing the reaction itself.

The application of Boric Acid itself in cases of infection of the bladder or renal pelvis, in single doses of 0.3-0.5 (daily doses of 1.2-2.0), was very much in vogue, especially in the eighties. This was introduced by GUYON, I believe.

---

[1] Attempts to increase the solubility by the admixture of magnesia (Scholtz, Massier) have been without success, so far as I know.

The results were generally considered favourable—if this treatment has been kept in the background in recent times, it is probably because we have since discovered more effective remedies (especially urotropin). My own experiences have been very satisfactory—I still occasionally use this remedy. That much prolonged or continually repeated use is by no means injurious, has been especially proved by one case, which I still often have occasion to observe. A superior officer, whose position requires him to undergo many bodily exertions, and by taking part in hunting, travelling, festivals, to frequently put up with a far from hygienic way of living, had suffered from chronic-atonic cystitis for 13 years. At first he took Boric Acid constantly for some weeks, then, on becoming better, left it off, but always had the remedy with him and took it again on the slightest relapse. His general health remained excellent, and he never observed the least unpleasant effect of this remedy, which he highly valued. The doses were 0·5 gramme each.

I have not much experience in the application of Borax in cases of acidity of the urine ; in general, I rather favour stronger alkalies. Even here, I have also frequently prescribed Boron, in the form of *magnesia boro-citrica*, likewise without ever observing any harm from this drug, even after continual use.

I remain, etc., etc.,

(Signed),   POSNER.

APPENDIX 5.

No. 1. **Artisan's Eczema of the Arms and Hands.**

F., FRANZ, 56 years old, mason. Patient maintains that he has always been in good health, and no illnesses have occurred in his family. His present complaint first appeared about 30 years ago. Patient then went to the Charité (hospital) for treatment and was dismissed in several weeks completely cured. In the course of the next few years, patient was repeatedly taken with the same complaint, which was sometimes confined to the upper extremities, sometimes affected the face and legs as well. An improvement took place each time after treatment, but only temporarily. Some four weeks ago the eruption appeared again, but in entirely altered form. Both hands, especially the right one, are slightly swollen. It is chiefly the back of the hand which is affected as far as the wrist, but some eruptions are also to be found on the forearm and fingers. The afflicted parts exhibit redness, a slight lustre, and numerous flat elevations as large as a lentil, which feel like hard knots. Unbearable itching continues, especially at night. Patient began treatment on December 6th, and the condition improved under the application of naphthalan, lenigallol, and menthol ointment, with the exception of a conjunctivitis, which he had often had previously. The treatment with Boric Acid began on December 27th, while the treatment with the ointment was continued. During the entire period of treatment with Boric Acid, the eczema diminished and the itching became less.

Date.	Boric Acid. grms.	URINE.		Remarks.
		Albumen.	Spec. weight.	
27 Dec., 1901	0·2	No albumen	1009	
28	0·2	,,	1004	
29	0·2	,,	1022	
30	0·2	,,	1015	
31	0·3	,,	1022	
1 Jan., 1902	0 3	,,	1019	
2	0·3	,,	1020	
3	0·3	,,	1021	
4	0·3	,,	1020	
5	0·3	,,	1022	
6	0·3	,,	1016	
7	1·0	,,	1021	
8	3·0	,,	1019	Appetite good; stools good.
9	3·0	,,	1019	,, ,,
10	3·0	,,	1019	,, ,,
11	3·0	,,	1018	,, ,,
12	3·0	,,	1021	,, ,,
13	3·0	,,	1019	,, ,,
14	3·0	,,	1018	,, ,,

APPENDIX 5—*continued*.

Date.	Boric Acid. grms	URINE.		Remarks.
		Albumen.	Spec. weight.	
15 Jan., 1902	—	No albumen.	1007	Complains of nausea, pains in the stomach; no stool. Dose stopped. Pains in the knees and neck.
16	3·0	,,	1016	Pains in neck, stomach, and knees continue. Nausea comes from throat, not from stomach. On examination great dryness of the throat is discovered, redness, symptoms of *pharyngitis sicca*. On examination of abdomen, liver found to be two finger-breadths below edge of ribs in right nipple line; the place is sensitive, as is also the left lobe of the liver. Pain in the stomach could not be detected. The stool was considerably retarded. Patient had procured purgative pills, which were without effect ; he received castor oil and a somewhat nourishing diet.
17	3·0	,,	1019	Pains in the stomach diminished, slight sensitiveness in the neighbourhood of the *flexura sigmoidea*. No nausea. Appetite somewhat better. Pains in the knees still present.
18	3·0	,,	1017	Angina improved. Pains in the knees continue, also somewhat in the stomach. Receives castor oil.
19	—	,,	1022	Pains all diminished. Castor oil taken effect (once).
20	—	,,	1015	Knocked his head in the dark passage. On the forehead is a swelling nearly as big as an apple, with an open wound nearly as big as a shilling piece. Has headache, pains in the stomach scarcely perceptible. More severe pains continue in the knees.
21	3·0	,,	1022	Pain in the stomach almost disappeared. Appetite and stools normal. Slight headache.
22	3·0	,,	1016	Health returned to normal.
1 Feb., 1902	—	...	—	Entirely good health, good appetite, regular stools. Flourishing appearance.

No. 2. **Rhagades of the Lower Lip.**

R., BERNHARD, 28 years old, tinker. Patient's brother has been suffering from pulmonary disease for two years; otherwise family history without importance for the diagnosis. Patient himself had measles at ten years; has suffered from rheumatism in the knees for the last four years; this always appears at changes of weather and lasts for about three days. Since the summer of 1901, patient has had a cough, in the autumn purulent sputum appearing, which was occasionally mixed with blood. At the same time patient noticed he was beginning to lose flesh. In October night-sweats occurred, which return almost every night since then. At the end of November a rhagade developed in the centre of the lower lip (patient is a great cigarette smoker). Infection is denied. The examination of the lungs has the following result: on the left side a slight weakness of resonance and jerking respiration in the *fossa supraspinata*; in the *fossa infraclavicularis* dry rhonchus. The treatment with Boric Acid begins on December 29th.

Date.	Borac Acid. grms.	URINE.		Remarks.
		Albumen.	Spec. Weight.	
28 Dec., 1901	—	—	—	The treatment of the rhagade begins with oxide of zinc plaster.
29	0·2	No albumen	1025	
30	0·2	,,	1026	
31	0 3	,,	1023	Rhagade begins to heal. Oxide of zinc mull plaster continued.
1 Jan , 1902	0·3	,,	1022	
2	0·3	,,	1021	
3	0·3	,,	1022	Lip further improved.
4	0·3	,,	1022	
5	0·3	,,	1012	
6	0·3	,,	1022	
7	1·0	,,	1022	
8	2 0	,,	1020	Lip healed. Patient complains of pains in both knees. Microscopic examination negative. *Spiritus sinapis.*
9	2·0	,,	1013	
10	8 0	,,	1024	
11	3·0	,,	1021	Slight redness on the forehead. Slight redness of the nose. Beginning of *folliculitis. Unguentum boricum* 25·0.
12	3 0	,,	1027	
13	3·0	,,	1026	
14	3·0	,,	1026	Twinges in the knees improved.
15	3 0	,,	1016	
16	3·0	,,	1021	
17	3 0	,,	1022	Forehead and nose improved.
18	3 0	,,	1028	Patient has a cold.
19	3·0	,,	1024	
20	—		—	Patient's general health has improved.

No. 8. Ulcus Durum Penis with Consecutive Bubo Inguinalis.

W., Gustav, 24 years, jailer. Patient's mother died of pleurisy; father alive and well, also four brothers and sisters. Patient has had *pleuritis costalis* and *pleuritis pulmonis* while a soldier; later one of his ribs underwent resection.

About the middle of December patient got an *ulcus durum* in the *sulcus coronarius*—four weeks after the infecting coition; the ulcer healed after a treatment of about a week with *europhen* (europhen 1·0, acid bor. 4·0). At the same time as the appearance of the ulcer, *bubo inguinalis* on the left side occurred, which was very painful from the beginning. Treatment with Boric Acid began on January 10th, 1902:—

Date.	Boric Acid. grms.	URINE.		Remarks.
		Albumen.	Spec. Weight.	
10 Jan., 1902	3·0	No albumen	1016	
11	3·0	,,	1013	
12	3·0	,,	1021	
13	3·0	,,	1022	
14	3·0	,,	1031	
15	3·0	,,	1022	
16	3·0	,,	1024	Bubo opened.
17	—	,,	—	Slight pain.
18	3·0	,,	1025	
19	3·0	,,	1023	Bandage changed, health otherwise good.
20	3·0	,,	1020	Bandage changed, wounds look well.
21	3·0	,,	1021	
22	—	—	—	
27	—	—	—	Bandage changed, wounds look well.
29	—	—	—	Health good.
31	—	—	—	Wounds look well. Ulcer entirely healed, no secondary symptoms.

No. 4. ## Ulcera Dura Penis.

Pr., Otto, 18 years, household servant, with the use of a tricycle. Patient's father died of pneumonia ; his mother is alive, but ailing. Brothers and sisters are alive and well. Patient asserts that he was well until about the end of November, 1901. At the end of November, a fortnight after the last cohabitation, he suffered from two ulcers in the penis, which both showed distinct hardening, and healed in a week from November 13th-20th under treatment with calomel. At the same time there was a painless *bubo inguinalis* on the left side, which, however, also went down after the ulcer healed. At about the end of December patient noticed a *bubo inguinalis sinister*, without feeling any pain ; the swelling became gradually larger, especially after patient cycling some few times. He received poultices of diluted *liquor plumbi subacetatis* on January 4th, 1902, under which treatment the swelling, which had been hard, softened. The Boric Acid treatment began on January 8th.

Date.	Boric Acid. grms.	URINE.		Remarks.
		Albumen.	Spec. Weight.	
8 Jan., 1902	8·0	No albumen	1017	
9	8·0	,,	1015	
10	8·0	.,	1017	
11	3·0	,,	1017	Stools retarded ; receives *pulv. liq. compositum*, a spoonful in the evening.
12	8·0	,,	1019	
13	3·0	,,	1014	More pain in walking, feeling of oppression. Bubo no larger.
14	3·0	,,	1019	
15	8·0	,,	1014	Pain less.
16	8·0	,,	1016	
17	8·0	,,	1012	
18	8·0	,,	1011	Stat. idem. Sandbag over the poultices, 4 lbs.
19	—	,,	1016	
21	—	—	—	Beginning of spotted eruption characteristic of lues on the body, especially on abdomen and chest, slighter on dorsum. (*Exanthema maculopapulosum*.) Vapour baths.
24	—	—	—	Syphilitic eruption worse. Vapour bath.
27	—	—	—	Syphilitic eruption worse. *Unguentum cinereum* 3·0g. Dos. X, 1 inunction daily.
31	—	—	—	Maculæ still worse.
4 Feb., 1902	—	—	—	The eruption has disappeared, the glandular swelling much diminished. On the right thigh is a slight eruption in consequence of the grey ointment.

No. 5. Glandular Swelling in the Submaxillary Region.

K., JOHANNES, 17 years, merchant's clerk. Parents and brothers and sisters of the patient are alive and well. Patient himself has suffered from " ulcers " several times, mostly in the face, also once in the arm ; he has always been well otherwise.

Towards the end of November, without external cause, a swelling, about the size of a lentil, appeared in the right submaxillary region, accompanied by a good deal of pain and redness. In the course of about a week a swelling nearly the size of a plum formed, causing violent twinges of pain. On being slightly compressed, pus came out of the swelling. Patient thereupon underwent a medical treatment. He received naphthalan mull plaster, under which a considerable secretion of pus soon formed, which led to noticeable diminution of the abscess.

Date.	Boric Acid. grms.	URINE.		Remarks.
		Albumen.	Spec. Weight.	
7 Jan., 1902	3·0	No albumen	1026	
8	3·0	,,	1022	Appetite good, stools normal.
9	3·0	,,	1026	
10	3·0	,,	1028	Further retrocession.
11	3·0	,,	1019	Still less swelling.
12	3·0	,,	—	
13	3·0	,,	1023	Very slight secretion.
14	3·0	,,	1024	
15	—	,,	—	Stopped.
16	3·0	,,	1030	Secretion disappeared, wound closed, gland considerably less swollen.
17	3·0	,,	1028	
18	3·0	,,	1024	
19	—	—	—	Perfectly normal.

No. 6.   Bubo Gummosus.

F., August, 48 years, mason. Patient's parents died from an unknown cause. Patient has only one sister, who is alive and well. Patient had typhoid fever some 30 years ago ; some 20 years ago he acquired a gonorrhœa, which healed in about three months. In 1897 he got a hard chancre, which disappeared shortly under treatment with iodoform. Four weeks after the chancre healed—in August, 1897—patient had eruptions over his whole body, and went to the Charité (hospital) ; there he received 37 injections with sublimate, whereupon the eruptions subsided. Then patient remained well for some time. At the end of 1900 he got two small ulcers in the penis again, which healed after treatment with a white ointment. In July, 1901, patient noticed several small swellings in the left inguinal region, which caused pain at first, especially in walking, but soon became painless. On September 1st he underwent a treatment with injections. He used 78 grms. of *unguentum cinereum*, but had to stop on account of ptyalism At the same time he took iodide of potassium, later tincture of iodine. Under this treatment the bubo gummosus soon subsided. But it speedily returned. Finally, a small opening formed on the summit of the bubo, from which a secretion continually escaped. Gradually violent fluctuation set in, so that on January 14th recourse was taken to incision. For over five years patient has also suffered from violent *acne rosacea* of the nose, which, according to his own statement, was sometimes better, sometimes worse. Lately, especially, some large nodes appeared on the nose, when it was complicated by a cold in the head. The treatment with Boric Acid began on January 13th, 1902.

Date.	Boric Acid grms.	URINE.		Remarks.
		Albumen.	Spec. Weight.	
13 Jan., 1902	4·0	No albumen	1017	
14	4·0	,,	1006	
15	—	.,	1021	Received no dose by mistake.
16	4·0	,,	1020	
17	4·0	,,	1018	
18	4·0	,,	1020	States the nose to be more inflamed ; has a cold in his head.
19	4·0	,,	1021	Cold continues ; tongue clean.
20	4·0	,,	1022	
27	—	—	—	Bandage changed ; wounds look well ; secrete less.
3 Feb., 1902	—	—	—	Bandage removed ; wounds secrete little ; zinc plaster.

No. 7. Ulcus Durum Laminæ Internæ Præputii with Consecutive Bubo Inguinalis.

F., CHRISTIAN, 27 years, turner. Patient maintains that he has always been well until now. He was married; a child, resulting from this marriage, is alive and well. About Christmas, 1901, patient noticed an ulcer on the lower side of the penis, presumably resulting from the last coition, which took place about the middle of November. He immediately put himself under medical treatment and received here on January 6th, 1902, calomel as a dusting powder for the ulcer, which was situated on the internal surface of the lower portion of the prepuce, and was moderately indurated, lardaceously covered, and pea-sized. The ulcer soon cleared. On January 11th patient got a *bubo inguinalis dexter* ; further inflammation of the prepuce set in, which caused acute *phymosis.* The urine was free from albumen, light yellow, and with acid reaction. The treatment with Boric Acid began the same day.

Date.	Boric Acid grms.	URINE.		Remarks.
		Albumen.	Spec. Weight.	
11 Jan., 1902	4·0			
12	4·0	No albumen	1026	
13	4·0	,,	1023	Bubo diminished. A slight inflammation of the prepuce continues, the swollen inguinal gland about the size of a plum, slightly sensitive to compression, painless in walking. The place of the ulcer feels hard through the prepuce.
14	4·0	,,	1024	
15	4·0	,,	1017	
16	4·0	,,	1025	
17	4·0	,,	1023	Bubo still painful. Inflammation of prepuce slighter.
18	—	,,	1021	Bubo slightly enlarged and reddened.
19	—	,,	—	Bubo still causes pain.

31

No. 8.   **Dermatitis after Scabies.**

G., MARIE, spinster, 28 years, ironer. Patient's parents and four brothers and sisters are alive and well. Three brothers and sisters died in early childhood, one sister, who appears to have been "consumptive," died at 10 years old. Patient had the measles at 8 years old. Nearly every year since her childhood she has suffered from eruptions of the skin on the face ; first the skin swells, then separate pustules appear up to the size of a sixpenny piece, which afterwards run together. They contained watery liquid, later suppuration set in. Patient treated herself with zinc vaseline. The eruption last appeared three years ago. Menstruation first occurred in her fifteenth year, and was not always regular. During the menses, patient usually suffers from nausea ; duration of a single menstruation, about a week. Six years ago patient had a normal delivery. She has an illicit connection. About the middle of November, patient was afflicted with a skin eruption, which spread over the whole body, but was specially violent on the abdomen. She underwent treatment on December 15th. Patient looks moderately well-fed. The affection proved to be *scabies*, turning to acute eczema through continual scratching. She received an innunction of balsamum Peruvianum with lanoline (1:10). On December 20th the itching had diminished considerably, while the traces of eczema were still present. The urine was free from albumen, spec. weight 1020, light yellow and transparent. The Borax treatment began.

Date.	Borax. grm.	URINE.		Remarks.
		Albumen.	Spec. Weight.	
20 Dec., 1901	0·2			
21	0·3	No albumen	1008	
23	0·8	,,	1022	
24	0·3	,,	1030	
26	0·8	,,	1019	
28	0·4	,,	1028	
29	0·4	,,	1027	
30	0·4	,,	1027	
31	0·5	,,	1026	
1 Jan., 1902	—	—	—	Patient did not appear.
2	0·5	,,	1025	Patient states she felt a chill at six o'clock in the afternoon.

No. 8—*continued.*

Date.	Borax. grm.	URINE.		Remarks.
		Albumen.	Spec. Weight.	
3 Jan., 1902	0·5	Albumen (?)	1034	Urine shows very slight opalescence on being boiled and having nitric acid added, which is lightened considerably by the addition of alcohol and ether; remains transparent on the addition of acetic acid and ferrocyanide of potash.
4	0·5	Albumen present.	1028	Urine shows extreme turbidness when boiled with nitric acid and ferrocyanide of potash. On centrifugalising the urine, a not inconsiderable sediment was left; this showed vesical epithelium under the microscope. Consequently, in order to obtain pure urine from the bladder, about 300 ccm. of urine was evacuated by means of the catheter in the afternoon; this was dark yellow, reacted very acidly, and showed slightly flaked turbidness. After centrifugalising, the deposit was examined under the microscope, and showed a considerable quantity of vesical epithelium, here and there leucocytes, but no casts.
5	0 5	,,	1021	Urine shows slight opalescence after boiling with nitric acid, likewise turbidness with acetic acid and ferrocyanide of potash, but distinctly less than in the urine of 4th Jan.
6	0·5	No albumen	1020	No turbidness of the urine when boiled with nitric acid, or with ferrocyanide of potash and acetic acid. The microscopic examination of the urine showed a remarkable diminution of the epithelial cells.
7	0·5	,,	1026	
8	—	,,	1026	Complains of violent pains in the face and head, has vomited. Violent migraine. Warm fomentations for the head ordered. Administration of Borax discontinued.

No. 8— *continued.*

Date.	Borax. grm.	URINE. Albumen.	Spec. Weight.	Remarks.
9 Jan., 1902	0·5	No albumen	1024	Same complaints, but diminished. No nausea. Warm fomentations continued.
10	0·5	,,	1027	Feels well, complains of nothing. Headache entirely gone.
11	0·5	.,	1030	
12	0·5	,,	1028	
13	0·5	,,	1022	
14	1·0*	,,	1024	
15	1·0*	,,	1028	Menstruation delayed.
16	—	—	—	Nausea after the second dose.
17	—	,,	1024	Administration of Borax interrupted on account of menstruation. Still slight itching on the arms. On the left upper arm a reddened swelling about the size of a hazelnut appears.
18	1·0*	,,	1024	General health improved.
19	1·0*	,,	1018	
20	1·0*	,,	1027	
21	0·5	.,		
22	—	—	—	A naphthalan plaster is ordered.
24	—	—	—	Itching disappeared. Abscess shows fluctuation.
25	—	—	—	Incision. Much pus comes out. Iodoform gauze bandage.
27	—	—	—	Bandage well placed, no pain.
31	—	—	—	Bandage changed. Wound looks well, secretes very little.
3 Feb., 1902	—	—	—	Bandage removed, nearly dry. Zinc mull plaster.
5	—	—	—	Wound is dry. Once a day oxide of zinc mull plaster.
17	—	—	—	States she is pregnant and concludes this from absence of menses, frequent nausea and change in general health.

* 0·5 grm. Morning and Evening.

34

No. 9.   **Artisan's Eczema of the Arms and Hands.**

L., ALFRED, 19 years, thick-set, looks pale. His parents and three brothers are alive and well; four brothers and sisters died in early youth, cause of death unknown. Patient suffered from *rhachitis* in his earliest childhood and did not learn to walk until his fourth year. He states that he has been entirely well, except for having had scarlet-fever in his fifth year. L. has been employed in looking after the machinery in the "Allgemeine Elektrizitäts-Gesellschaft" since 1900. Patient states he first suffered from an eruption on the right arm in July, 1901. It began in the region of the wrist and spread as far as the elbow-joint. The extension side was chiefly affected. A week later he got the same sort of eruption on the left arm, but here it was confined to the elbow-joint. The treatment he then received consisted of a white ointment, the ingredients of which could not be stated. It took about four weeks to heal. At the beginning of November, 1901, an eruption again appeared on the right arm; it began in the middle of the forearm and spread to the wrist and elbow. This time the eruption was discharging, the skin much inflamed and inclined to bleed. On the application of zinc ointment, which he prescribed himself, no improvement occurred. He therefore underwent treatment on November 25th. On the application of external remedies, such as *liquor aluminii acetici*, later *ichthargan cintment* 0·3:15 and *pasta zinci*, an improvement occurred. The Borax treatment began on December 21st.

Date.	Borax. grm.	URINE.		Remarks.
		Albumen.	Spec. Weight.	
21 Dec., 1901	0·3			
23	0·3	No albumen	1023	Only a very slight redness shows; the swelling is almost entirely gone.
24	0·3	,,	1013	
26	0·3	,,	1018	
27	0·3	,,	1029	
28	0·4	,,	1021	
29	0·4	,,	1023	
30	0·4	,,	1020	
31	0·5	,,	1022	
1 Jan., 1902	0·5	,,	1022	

No. 9—*continued.*

Date.	Borax. grms.	URINE.		Remarks.
		Albumen.	Spec. Weight	
				Two days' pause for external reasons.
4 Jan., 1902	0·5	No albumen	1012	
5	0·5	,,	1021	
6	0·5	,,	1024	
7	0·5	,.	1012	
8	1·0	,,	1014	
9	1·0	,,	1012	
10	1·0	,,	1020	
11	2·0	,,	1012	
12	2·0	,,	1011	
13	2·0	,,	1020	
14	2·0	,,	1023	
15	2·0	,,	1020	
16	2·0	,,	1016	
17	2·0	,,	1009	
18	2·0	,,	1018	
19	2·0	,,	1012	
20	2·0	,.	1019	Health good, as was always the case.
21	—	,,	1028	
22	2·0	,,	1026	
23	2·0	,,	1021	
24	2·0	,,	—	
26	2·0	,.	1024	
27	2·0	,,	1022	

D 2

No. 10.   Pityriasis Rosea.

PA., OTTO, apprentice, 16 years, has only had measles as a child. Parents alive and well; three brothers and sisters, aged 20—25, also well. Three sisters and brothers, from 2—3 years old, deceased; patient does not know of what illness.. Patient has had neither scrofula nor any other disease. At the beginning of December, 1901, he was affected with pruritus on the chest and back. On December 11th patient consulted a physician, who prescribed rubbing with balsam of Peru and soap baths, but the cutaneous eruption and the itching continued. Patient began treatment on December 14th. On admission, a great number of small papulose efflorescences appeared on the chest, abdomen, back, and thighs. Further, some small papulæ, varying from the size of a pea to a sixpenny piece, appeared, being slightly squamous in the centre. With the exception of these few places, the whole affection made the impression of an irritation caused by soap baths taken formerly. The following was prescribed: Peruol 5·0, lauoline 45·0. On December 16th the itching had diminished, on the 18th it had further decreased, the skin looked less red; the separate places were still distinctly recognisable as *pityriasis rosea*. The Borax treatment began on December 20th.

Date.	Borax.	URINE.		Remarks.
	grm.	Albumen.	Spec. Weight.	
20 Dec., 1901	0·2			
21	0·3	No albumen	1020	Itching only felt at night.
23	0·3	,,	1018	
24	0·3	,.	1022	
26	0·3	,,	1023	
27	0·3	,.	1027	Some fresh *pityriasis rosea* efflorescences appear on the flexor side of both forearms.
28	0·4	,,	1016	
29	0·4	,,	1026	
30	0·4	A trace of albumen	1023	
31	0·5	No albumen	1013	
1 Jan., 1902	0·5	,,	—	
2	0·5	,,	1021	The conditions on the arm retrocede, itching less on the whole.

No. 10—*continued.*

		URINE.		Remarks.
Date.	Borax. grms.	Albumen.	Spec. Weight.	
3 Jan., 1902.	0·5	—	1026	Urine shows very slight opalescence when boiled with nitric acid, clearing almost entirely on the admixture of alcohol and ether. On admixture of acetic acid and ferrocyanide of potash more turbidness, which only clears slightly on the admixture of alcohol and ether.
4	0·5	Entirely free from albumen	1014	
5	0·5	No albumen	1021	
6	0·5	,,	1018	Absolutely transparent urine again.
7	0·5	,,	1026	
8	1·0	,,	1019	
9	1·0	,,	1025	
10	2·0	.,	1021	
11	2·0	,,	1025	
13	3·0	,,	1022	
14	3·0	,,	1027	
15	3·0	,,	1016	
16	3·0	,,	1016	
17	3·0	,,	1020	Looks well.
18	3·0	,,	1023	
20	3·0	,,	1026	Healed, with the exception of some small squamous spots on the forearm.
21	3·0	,,	1021	
22	3·0	,,	1022	
23	3·0	,,	1021	
24	3·0	,,	1016	
25	3·0	,,	1019	Feels well.
26	3·0	,,	1021	
27	3·0	,,	1013	
28	3·0	,,	1024	
29	3·0	,,	—	
30	—	—	—	Feels well, no complaints.
2 Feb., 1902	—	—	—	Last traces of the eruption disappeared 8 days ago.

No. 11. Washerwoman's Eczema.

L., ELISE, spinster, 23 years, washerwoman. Patient's parents died of pulmonary phthisis; one brother died of paralysis of the heart, other sisters and brothers died in early childhood, except one sister, who is alive and well. Patient was scrofulous as a child, but otherwise always well. At about the middle of September, 1901, she was affected with a running eruption on both hands, which hindered her greatly in her work. She put herself into the hands of a doctor on September 17th. An improvement occurred gradually under treatment with naphthalan ointment, so that she was dismissed as cured in the middle of December, 1901. In the middle of January, however, the complaint returned, making a repetition of the treatment with naphthalan necessary. The eruption showed on both forearms, especially on the lower part, and proved to be *eczema papulo-vesiculosum et madidans infiltratum* arranged in patches varying from the size of a shilling to that of the palm of the hand. The itching was rather violent, so that the effect of scratching was plainly visible in several places. Menstruation had not occurred for the last two years. The Borax treatment began on January 15th, 1902.

Date.	Borax. grms.	URINE.		Remarks.
		Albumen.	Spec. Weight.	
15 Jan., 1902	1·0			
16	1·0	No albumen	1026	
17	2·0*	,,	1026	
18	2·0*	,,	1030	
19	1·0	,,	1026	
20	2·0*	,,	1020	Improvement.
21	2·0*	,,	1023	
22	2·0*	,,	1025	Further improvement.
23	2·0*	,,	1023	Appearance decidedly fresher.
24	2·0*	,,	1024	
25	2·0*	,,	1023	
26	1·0	,,	1020	
27	2·0*	,,	1020	Further improvement. Fomentations with *liquor aluminii acetici*.
28	2·0*		1022	
29	—	—	—	Redness of the forearm increased. Naphthalan administered again.
30	—	—	—	Feels entirely well, appearance almost flourishing.

* Morning and Evening 1·0 gramme respectively.

No. 12. Injury of the Arms and Hands from Solution of Caustic Soda.

M., LUISE, Mrs., 44 years. Patient's father died by his own hand ; mother died of old age ; three brothers and sisters alive and well. Patient's husband deceased of pneumonia ; three children are sound. Patient herself has frequently suffered from pneumonia, but was otherwise constantly in good health. Menstruation first appeared in her sixteenth year, and was always regular, until it stopped some six months ago, and has not recurred since. The births were always normal.

Towards the beginning of December, 1901, patient noticed violent itching and burning in her hands, after she had wiped up a solution of caustic soda, which had run over (she is employed at a chemical factory) ; soon after a vesicular eruption set in, which discharged freely and spread over the forearm. She put herself in the hands of a doctor and received a white ointment, the composition of which could not be ascertained. No improvement or alleviation of the complaint followed. In the treatment on January 12th, 1902, she received first fomentations of *liquor aluminii acetici*, after which the running and eruption decreased slightly on the whole. On January 15th she received talcum for the night and chamomile fomentations for the day ; under this treatment (January 20th) the eruption diminished considerably.

Date.	Borax. grms.	URINE. Albumen.	Spec. Weight	Remarks.
15 Jan., 1902	1·0	—	—	Patient received talcum and chamomile fomentations.
16	1·0	No albumen	1009	
17	2·0*	,,	1009	
18	2·0*	,,	1019	
19	—	,,	1017	(Sunday.) Patient came too late.
20	2·0*	,,	1014	Under this treatment the eruption decreased considerably. In the daytime continued, at night naphthalan.
21	2·0*	,,	1020	

* Morning and Evening 1·0 gramme respectively.

40

No. 12—*continued.*

| Date. | Borax. grms. | URINE. | | Remarks. |
		Albumen.	Spec. Weight	
22 Jan., 1902	1·0	No albumen	1013	Patient complains of headache and pains in the joints, a condition which has often occurred during change of weather. Becomes worse after naphthalan, pustule formation begins. Only fomentations with *liquor aluminii acetici*, 1 dessert spoonful (15 grammes) in ¼ litre of water.
23	2·0*	,,	1012	Condition considerably improved. The pustules have opened, eczema better. Treatment continued.
24	2·0*	..	1015	
25	2·0*	,,	1017	Improvement. Fomentations continued.
26	1·0	,.	1018	
27	2·0*	,,	1020	Improvement. Treatment continued.
28	2·0*	,.	1020	
29	1·0	,.	—	Improvement. Treatment continued.
30	—	—	—	Patient complains of headache and twinges in the joints.
1 Feb., 1902	—	—	—	Feels entirely normal again.
3	---	—	—	Only slight moisture.
5	—	—	—	Moisture disappeared, redness less.

* Morning and Evening 1·0 gramme respectively.

Plate I

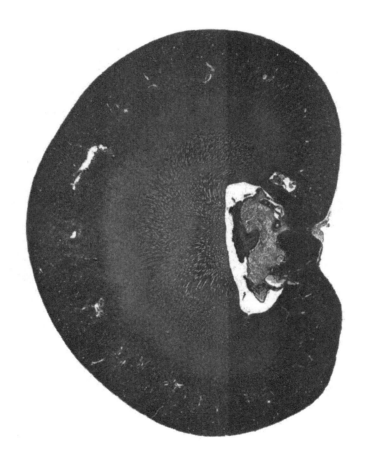

Rabbit's Kidney after Injection.

Plate
Table II.

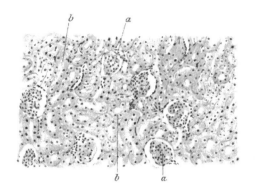

Normal.

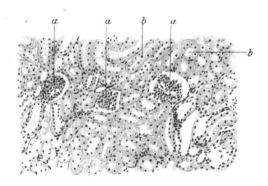

Normal after Injection.

Plate
Table III.

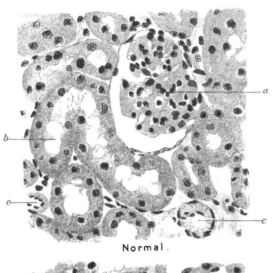

Normal.

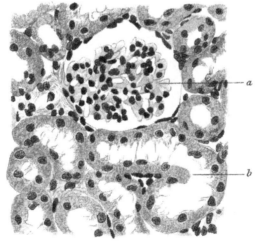

Normal after Injection.

a. *Glomeruli.*
b. *Tubuli Uriniferi.*
c. *Blood Vessels.*

Liebreich II.

Plate
~~Table~~ IV

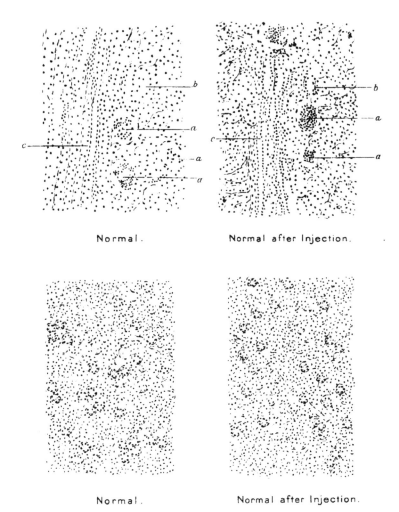

Normal.   Normal after Injection.

Normal.   Normal after Injection.

a *Glomeruli*.
b *Tubuli Contorta*.
c *Tubuli recti*.

Liebreich II

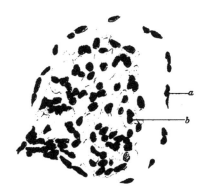

Normal.

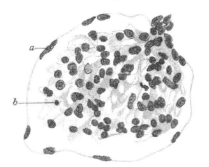

Normal after Injection.

a. *Renal Capsule Epithelium.*
b. *Cells of Glomerulus.*

SUPPLEMENT I.

TO THE

SECOND TREATISE

ON THE

EFFECTS OF

BORAX AND BORIC ACID.

BY

DR. OSCAR LIEBREICH,

O. Ö. PROFESSOR DER UNIVERSITÄT BERLIN UND GEHEIMER MEDIZINALRAT.

BERLIN, 1902.

SUPPLEMENT I.

Shortly after I had collected these observations, the proclamation of February 18th, 1902, concerning injurious and deceptive admixtures in meat and its preparations, appeared, which contains the following clauses:—

"In pursuance of the decisions of par. 21 of the law of June "3rd, 1900 (Reichs-Gesetzbl., p. 547), with regard to the official "inspection of cattle and meat, the Federal Council (Bundesrat) "has passed the following statutes:—

"The provisions of par. 21, section 1, of the law are applicable "to the following substances, as well as to the substances used in "their preparation :

"Boric Acid and its salts, etc."

From this ordinance it follows that the prohibition only refers to such things as must be considered meat in the meaning of the law.

On February 24th, 1902, the following paragraph was published in the "Deutscher Reichsanzeiger":

"The draft, upon which the Bundesrat founded the resolution "on injurious and deceptive ingredients in meat and preparations "thereof, according to par. 21 of the statute relating to the public "inspection of meat, and which was made public by the Chancellor "on February 18th, 1902 (Reichs-Gesetzbl., p. 48), was accompanied "by a technical argument, the material contents of which we give "as follows."[1]

As the essential points are emphasized, it is possible to judge of the subject, even without knowing the entire contents of the draft.

In the third column, the special part, viz. "Boric Acid and its Salts," begins. Near the commencement the following statement appears :—

"The first Boron preservative for meat and milk, which came "on the market, was the so-called 'aseptine' (1873). There are "now a large number of Boron preservatives, etc."

First appearance of Boron preservatives.

---

[1] "Deutscher Reichsanzeiger u. Königlich Preussischer Staatsanzeiger," February 24th, 1902.

From these words, one is led to suppose that no Boron preservative existed or was used in the trade previous to aseptine. But this is not the case In fact, the date "1873" is not correct as regards aseptine, which was already known in the year 1870.[1] But Boron preparations came into the trade even earlier, for SPEAR in Ixelles (Belgium) took out a patent in 1867 for preservation by Boric Acid or Boric Acid and sulphuric acid. Moreover, directions for the preservation of milk extract[2] existed as early as the year 1861. One of them runs thus:—

Extractum Lactis.	English.
Rp. Lactis vaccini recentis P. 1500.	Fresh milk 1500 parts.
Natrii carbonici cryst. P. 1.	Crystallized soda 1 part.
Boracis P. 1.	Borax 1 part.
Sacchari albi P. 5.	White sugar 5 parts.
Mixtas leni calore ad extracti tertii gradus consistentiam evaporando redige.	The mixture to be evaporated by gently heating, to a thick extract.

HAGER even asserts that the preservative quality of Borax for milk is "*an old and well-known fact*,"[3] and especially in northern countries Borax has been largely applied for the preservation of food long before the use of aseptine. This must be mentioned, because we thus get a different view, as opposed to the assertion that in the case of Borax and Boric Acid we have to do with one of the most recent products for the preservation of food. It is important to emphasize this, because the opinion is asserted in the technical argument, *as though Boron preparations*, in contrast to the application of saltpetre, *were a new kind of preservative*, founded only on short, and therefore less weighty, experience.

We will first study those assertions of the technical argument which are intended to prove the injuriousness of Boron preparations:

Alleged difference between the supposed irritative effect of Borax and Boric Acid on the mucous membrane.

It is stated that "Borax, which has an alkaline reaction, more easily causes "irritation and redness of the mucous membrane of the stomach and intes- "tines, oppression, nausea, and vomiting than Boric Acid." It is not apparent, either from literature or scientific labours, upon what grounds it is proved that either preparation causes irritation and especially redness of the

---

[1] "Archiv der Pharmacie." Vol. 200. No. 1, p. 45.

[2] "Pharmaceutische Centralhalle." Vol. 12 (1871), p. 296.

[3] "H. Hager, Manuale Pharmaceuticum." II. Edit., 1861, Vol. I., p. 148.

mucous membrane of the stomach and intestines, for no case of poisoning exists, nor even a case in which Borax was taken by chance before death, in which a discovery justifying this conclusion was made at the post-mortem examination. No experiments on animals have had this result either, as I have already explained in my first treatise.

It is granted further that Boric Acid may be considered a " compara- " tively harmless substance " in connection with the irritation of the mucous membrane; but it is not apparent for what reason it is only " comparatively " harmless. Boron preparations are *absolutely* harmless to the mucous membrane; in fact, it is stated in the following sentence that " neither on the " ocular conjunctiva, nor the mucous membrane of the cavity of the mouth, " the stomach, the intestines or the bladder has even a saturated solution " of 4 per cent. shown an injurious effect on human beings." The correctness of this sentence in the technical argument has become known from the abundant literature on the subject. I have also mentioned that even large doses prove of beneficial effect on the mucous membrane. So that the word " comparatively " is entirely unfounded. Moreover, the remarks as to " comparative harmlessness " entirely contradict the statements quoted in the paragraph before. Therefore it is not of the least importance that Dr. Röse's case[1], which is quite isolated and is probably not the result of Borax at all, is cited against it in the technical argument. Further, it is a proved fact that Borax is one of the most useful remedies in cases of affections of the mucous membrane of the mouth. If we were to allow one such isolated case to be taken as a proof in the biological sciences, we could turn every physical truth upside down.

Dr. Röse writes:—" Borax caused, for instance, in the case of my wife, a painful inflammation of the mouth and throat with bluish-red mucous membrane and lasting for several days." From this one experiment, and in the face of an overwhelming number of observations to the contrary, Dr. Röse actually comes to the conclusion that not only Borax but *also* Boric Acid causes this phenomenon in general, although he *can give no instance at all* applying to Boric Acid. Evidently in Mrs. Röse's case the mucous membrane must have been in a condition such as has never as yet been observed in any person, and even should another case, coinciding with this one, be discovered, it would prove nothing against the application of Borax, since here a pathological condition, either known or unknown, must have been present to cause this abnormal effect. The opinion that Borax is poisonous

---

[1] " Zeitschr. f. Hygiene u. Infektionskrankheiten." Vol. 36, 1901, p. 184.

to cells, may also be considered as refuted by the experiments on epithelium in my first treatise.

I must also mention the assertion that an increased disintegration of the cells of the intestinal wall takes place. This hypothesis has been completely refuted in my first treatise, which is founded on direct experiments on the effect of Borax and Boric Acid on the mucous membrane itself. It is surprising, therefore, that an experiment of RÖSE's, which is by no means conclusive, should again be referred to in this connection.

Concerning digestive derangements, the "Gutachten des deutschen Fleischerverbandes" is cited. This article makes a distinction between Boric Acid and Borax, which, with respect to their effect on the human body, are in general considered to be identical, and contains the assertion that meat containing Borax is indigestible ; but we cannot consider the opinion of a Butchers' Union as authoritative on the digestibility of meat, for no hygienic or medical authority was to be found in the Union at that time.

If now my experiments (1. c. p. 10) are cited as proving an irritation of the mucous membrane of the stomach, *this is entirely unjustifiable*. The technical argument runs as follows :—

> " Thus LIEBREICH found that in the case of two of the dogs " experimented upon by him, to which he daily administered " 0·23 to 0·24 grm. of Boric Acid per kilo of body weight (*i.e.*, a " quantity far below that given by NEUMANN as within the limits " of innocuousness for dogs), there was vomiting after 12 and 15 " days respectively."

This citation is incorrect, because it is *not quoted in full*, and therefore does not justify a conclusion, for in the same paragraph of my treatise it is stated, "After 36 *days of feeding, no unfavourable change* in general health had taken place," and if the accompanying Appendix No. 1 of my first treatise be referred to it will be found that vomiting only occurred to dog A on April 4th, and, *during the continued feeding with Boric Acid until April 28th, never occurred again*. Likewise in the case of dog B, vomiting only occurred on April 6th, and *during the continued feeding with Boric Acid until April 28th* no more vomiting occurred. Dog A even increased in weight by 260 grammes, the decrease in weight of dog B being scarcely noticeable. Neither did I assert the vomiting to be a result of Boric Acid, but only mentioned that although dogs often vomited after the usual feeding, yet we would consider this as caused by the Boric Acid, a statement serving to show how objectively these experiments are conducted.

On the other hand, the following experiment, which was made in the Kaiserliches Gesundheitsamt, cannot be considered as conclusive. It was as follows :—

> "A dog weighing 10 kilogrammes vomited after 2 grammes of "Boric Acid in its usual meat food, although it had taken doses of "carbonate of soda up to 8 grammes, nitrate of potash (saltpetre) "up to 10 grammes, and could not even bear the amount of "1 gramme of Boric Acid, in 100 ccm. of water, fasting, although "it did not vomit before or after on plain water."

Inconclusive experiment on a dog.

The answer to this is simply that a dog, the *gastric mucous membrane of which is already injured* by carbonate of soda and saltpetre, must naturally be considered abnormal, for its mucous membrane is altered by the substances already applied in immoderate quantities. For according to the experiments[1] noted in my first treatise, it must be considered proved that, in the case of soda, an injurious effect on the mucous membrane of the stomach is recognisable after a solution of 1 per cent.; in the case of saltpetre the injurious effect on the stomach begins with a solution of only $\frac{1}{2}$ per cent., and likewise on the mucous membrane of the stomach. The dog used for the experiment in the Kaiserliches Gesundheitsamt was thus, so to say, predisposed for vomiting. Even if long intervals elapsed between administering saltpetre and carbonate of soda (which is not stated), this experiment cannot be considered decisive, since it is not evident whether the epithelium had recovered its normal condition.

MATTERN's experiments, which are mentioned further on in the same paragraph, in which he took 1 gramme of Boric Acid without bad effects, and felt violent pains in the stomach after 2 grammes, likewise BINSWANGER's experiments, cannot be cited as a proof of the injurious properties of Boric Acid ; they are isolated cases as opposed to the large number of experiments in which Boric Acid had done no harm. Especially MACNAUGHTON's case, previously quoted, contradicts it, for he took as much as 3 grammes Borax in solid form without an injurious effect being occasioned. But it is a wrong

Mattern's experiments with Boric Acid.

---

[1] See First Treatise, p. 36, or "Vierteljahresschr," 3rd Series. XIX., 1., p. 108.

principle altogether in this question *to examine an ingredient of food by itself without the food, or diluted with water or other things.* No one would care to make such an experiment with ground mustard or pepper. This holds good even for common salt ; the salt used in preparing food usually does not agree with people when drunk only diluted with water. Why, solution of common salt is used as an emetic !

In judging of the hygienic value of Boron compounds, one cannot cite the increase of an irritation of the stomach and intestines, which was already present. There are numberless kinds of food, which cause the same symptoms without the addition of preservatives.

If, as the " technical argument " further states, " there have been cases in England lately in which infants have suffered from diarrhœa after being fed with preserved milk," this would, of course, require special attention, should the statements prove true, for they have only been made lately, and it would certainly be desirable that when Borax is added to milk, a declaration to this effect should be enforced by law. As a proof that Borax and Boric Acid have not a purgative effect, we may mention MacNaughton's case on page 14, in which Borax and Boric Acid caused no stomach trouble whatever, even in concentrated form and swallowed with water.

The assertion that a special danger exists in consequence of Boric Acid being eliminated from the system slowly, has already been refuted in this treatise. I wish to call attention to the fact that some experiments are not quite decisive, because the food has not been examined for Boron preparations. Mistakes may easily arise from this cause.

That Boric Acid has been found in the urine of persons suffering from kidney disease after six or eight weeks, seems by no means strange, consider- ing that everything which is eaten, and even products of the body, are retained, for the simple reason that the kidneys are more impassable. But that the Boric Acid retained caused a disturbance in the system, has not been proved, nor. consequently, the statement in the technical argument, " that Boric Acid has a chronic effect." For it is impossible to judge of food from the standpoint of its agreeing with persons having kidney disease. It is especially incorrect to assert that the *protracted appearance* of Boric Acid in the urine *has a chronic effect* when no special abnormal symptoms appear in the system, these latter, in fact, being absent.

49

The favourable observation cited as to the reception of Borax and Boric Acid by human beings, is by no means exhaustively given. *The cases in which Borax agrees well are certainly too numerous* to be all mentioned ; nevertheless, more should have been referred to in order to form a judgment.

In spite of this it seemed of importance to study KISTER's case, which is cited in proof of a pathological effect, as has been done in this treatise (p. 5).

The experiments on cats, which are referred to in the same paragraph, have already been adversely criticised in this treatise (see p. 4).

On the comparison that saltpetre was given to a dog in the Reichs-gesundheitsamt without difference in weight being caused, while in my experiments on dogs a difference occurred, it must be remarked that no decisive value can be set on the weight in either of these experiments ; on the other hand, it must be pointed out how injuriously saltpetre may affect the epithelium, although it is constantly used as an ingredient in food in proper quantities without objection.

<small>Comparison between Saltpetre and Boron compounds.</small>

Concerning the occurrence of cutaneous eruptions, it is even admitted that the observations on the subject are not "unexceptionable." I allow that eruptions of the skin are occasionally observed after medicinal application, especially in large quantities. This occurs after a great number of substances which we occasionally take, but especially after eatables, such as strawberries, lobster, crab, etc., and these eruptions have already been mentioned in my first treatise (see p. 3) when discussing idiosyncrasies. Therefore it is entirely unjustifiable that, nevertheless, three cases are mentioned, which were published chiefly on account of their exceptional character and which cannot be regarded as representing the effects peculiar to Boric Acid. For instance, one is as follows :—

<small>Cutaneous eruptions.</small>

> "And HANDFORD communicated an observation lately, in
> "which only Boric Acid could have been the cause of the cutaneous
> "eruption ; moreover, an eruption occurred in the case of a patient
> "suffering from dilatation of the stomach every time that the
> "stomach was irrigated with a solution of Boric Acid, but not
> "when plain water was used."

Attention must be drawn to the fact that here and also in BINSWANGER's case, which is again referred to in the technical argument, the matter is different. In my first treatise on page 8 it reads thus :—

<small>Binswanger's experiment on himself.</small>

E.

" A series of experiments were made on himself by BINS-
" WANGER to test the effect of Boric Acid. He took 5 grains of Boric
" Acid fasting, noticed no effect during the forenoon, took four
" more doses of 5 grains each two hours apart during the afternoon,
" and finally the last dose at eight o'clock p.m., *i.e.*, more than 18
" decigrammes in all, without any other effect—as the author
" himself says—than that he enjoyed his supper famously. It was
" not until he had increased the dose tenfold that it began to
" disagree with him. A drachm (3·654 grammes) was taken
" without producing abnormal symptoms. It was only when a
" second drachm was taken, after two hours' interval, that vomiting
" set in. A third dose having been taken in the course of the
" afternoon, he again vomited ; after a couple of hours, however, he
" completely regained his normal condition."

It will thus be seen that the enormous dose of 7·3 grammes was taken
here, or rather in all 10·96 grammes, which is altogether out of comparison
with the quantities used in the ordinary way in food preserving. Likewise,
in HANDFORD's case, it was a question of a strong solution for irrigation.
Concerning irrigation of the stomach, it may be seen from a number of other
treatises that the stomach has been washed out thousands of times without
such a phenomenon occurring. I think I ought to refer to HANDFORD's
words here, who says, concerning a case of diarrhœa, which is supposed to
have occurred after Borax[1] :—

" That is my opinion, but I do not wish to bring forward that
" *one case as a crucial one*."

That cutaneous eruptions are not an integral part of the effect of Borax,
has been proved by the cases published in my second treatise. Besides, as
unnecessarily large doses of Borax have imprudently been used for preservation, public attention would be drawn to the sudden appearance of cutaneous
eruptions, seemingly without any special cause.

As regards the assertion that a *distinct* interference with the process of
assimilation is caused, and that this objection was raised by me in the case of

---

[1] Report of the Departmental Committee appointed to inquire into the use of preservatives
and colouring matters in the preservation and colouring of food, together with minutes of
evidence, appendices, and index. London, 1901, p. 78.

51

the dog also, this is again incorrectly quoted, for in my treatise it is stated as follows :—

"It seems certain, therefore, that an increase—*though hardly* "*an important one* —of the nitrogenous contents of fæces takes place "when Borax or Boric Acid is taken in food." (See further in the first treatise, p. 15.)

Besides this, experiments were made subsequently by LEBBIN[1] on human beings in connection with assimilation, which resulted in favour of normal assimilation. A more or less decreased assimilation, moreover, probably takes place in the case of all preserved foods, and surely cannot lead to the preserving of foods being altogether prohibited by legislation, for the loss in nutritive value must be so slight as not to find expression in the price. *Preservation by Boric Acid preparations is, above all, not an administrative, but an hygienic question.*

Now in regard to the experiments of ROST, who found a decrease of body weight in human beings ; the loss of body weight is not fully confirmed by RUBNER's experiments, the explanation being given that the persons experimented upon by RUBNER were undergoing a fattening treatment during the normal period. It is difficult to decide whether this explanation is correct or not ; at any rate, ROST's experiments have found no confirmation so far, and it is scarcely possible to consider such experiments authoritative, contrasted with the very long experience which exists regarding food containing Boric Acid. The large quantities of Borax and Boric Acid found in preserved food, according to the technical argument, would, considering the enormous consumption of borated meat, have caused people to notice an effect on their own health, for a person could scarcely bear such a continual decrease of weight for a fortnight without injury to the health. If it be borne in mind how many contingencies may arise in determining the weight of human beings, these alone cannot be of any importance in the face of practical experience. I will mention here that one of my patients, even after taking 60·9 grms. in 37 days, felt *particularly fresh,* and that the general health of all the others had distinctly improved. It must be reserved for later experiments to revert to these observations of ROST ; in any case they cannot be considered decisive.

Loss of weight after food containing Borax.

Very interesting are RUBNER's experiments, which were published on February 15th, 1902, that is, four days before the decree of the Bundesrat was

Rubner's experiments metabolism.

[1] Medizinische Woche, 1901. No. 38.

E 2

issued. These experiments prove, according to the technical argument, an injurious effect on the quantity of fat and of water in the system. Opposed to these experiments stand the practical results of TUNNICLIFFE and ROSENHEIM, that children increased in weight on a diet containing Borax and Boric Acid. Through this single experiment of RUBNER'S an objection was raised shortly before the promulgation of the law, which objection is in no way supported by practical experience.

It is right, of course, that the result of experimental work be referred to, in order to judge of the effect of *newly introduced* substances, when experience is wanting; but in Borax we have a preservative which has long been in use, the application of which, in very large doses, has also served for medical purposes, with the result, as I explained in both my treatises, that its innocuousness is proved. Should experimental objections be raised here, they must be particularly carefully discussed, for our biological methods are not so accurate as to be able to overturn the experience of years, and serve principally and generally as a scientific support of experience. It must also be emphasized that no absolute conclusions are admissible after a single series of experiments of such short duration, particularly with experiments on metabolism which in themselves call for strict criticism, especially in the case of human beings.

The importance in experiments on metabolism of examining the substance in question for a *considerable number of days*, is proved by the experiments of ROSEMANN[1], " Ueber die Wirkung des Alkohols auf den Eiweissstoffwechsel," and R. O. NEUMANN[2], " Ueber die Wirkung des Alkohols als Eiweisssparer." In the first four and six days respectively, the alcohol, which was added to the usual diet, effected, if anything, an increased assimilation of albumen ; it was not until the fifth and seventh days respectively that the consumption of albumen and fat decreased, that is, that it had the effect of *economising albumen and fat*, which effect continued to the end (the tenth and fourteenth days respectively). Had the experiments been broken off after the first days, only the (seemingly !) injurious effect on the absorption of material by alcohol would have been noticed. RUBNER'S experiments seem, therefore, to have lasted too short a time.

Whoever considers the experience in the application of Boron preparation, cannot be blind to the fact that it has frequently been opposed by

---

[1] Pflüger's Arch. 86, 307.
[2] Archiv f. Hygiene 41, 85.

medical men who must be designated *purists*, *i.e.*, whose principle it is that no preservatives whatever should be added to food. The reasons for this certainly very idealistic principle cannot, however, be considered very pertinent. They say, in general, that all sorts of injuries may accompany the use of such drugs—slight complaints such as headache, diarrhœa, stomach-ache, and nervous disturbances; but one may rightly retort that the appearance of these several symptoms can only be ascribed to the drug when it is medically proved to be connected with the preserved food taken; and we must bear in mind that when a substance is injurious, certain symptoms of the disease must be present, which may vary perhaps in detail, but must remain the same on the whole. If we wish to trace these symptoms to any preservative, we must understand that these symptoms very often occur in people whose food supply is altogether stinted, that is, in poor people. But not only the poor will suffer from it; wealthy people will also lose many appetising dishes through the prohibition of preservatives. Some people can bear tongue preserved with Borax, even after digestive derangements, excellently, while they are obliged to refuse ordinary salted tongue.

In consequence of the present widely-circulated medical assistance granted to all sufferers by the sick-fund legislation, and provided even for the poor of cities by the Poor-Law Medical Officers, doctors have an opportunity, when disturbances occur after taking injurious matters, of tracing the symptoms to specific causes. The experts for this are to be sought for among the doctors, for we know that many important hygienic questions have been brought into discussion entirely by the doctors and not by the hygienists themselves. Besides, illnesses occurring from the use of preservatives, even the slight complaints before mentioned, would become chronic during a continuation of the diet, or, should the diet be altered, would return when the preservative was again made use of, a fact which could scarcely have escaped the notice of doctors or patients. But it would exceed the limits of this treatise to examine all these objections. The length to which these purists go is best seen from Professor Halliburton's words[1] :—

> " 7573. And that with regard to the other preservatives, if " they were labelled, that would meet your objection; is that your " position generally ?—H. : No. I feel that the ideal condition of " things would be to prohibit them all."

[1] Report of the Departmental Committee appointed to enquire into the use of preservatives and colouring matters in the preservation and colouring of food, together with minutes of evidence appendices, and index. London, 1901, p. 265.

"7575. All preservatives?—H. : All preservatives."

"7576. Would you prohibit nitrate of potash, too ?—H. : Yes
" One knows, even from smoking cigarettes, that nitrate of potash
" is not absolutely harmless." [1]

Were we to give way to these principles, the consequence would be, as HALLIBURTON wishes, that the numberless preservatives, which have been in use for years, would be put under a veto.

It is altogether inadmissible to reject substances, which experience has proved innocuous, in consequence of isolated scientific examinations or isolated observations.

Possible difficulties for the sanitary police arising from the impossibility of distinguishing Borax and Boric Acid by analysis, can be overcome by only indicating the quantity of Boric Acid which is to be considered permissible.

---

[1] For most readers it is unnecessary to remark that in inhaling cigarette smoke, *not saltpetre but the injurious matters formed by its decomposition*, are inhaled, as in the case of gunpowder.

SUPPLEMENT II.

TO THE

SECOND TREATISE

ON THE

EFFECTS OF
BORAX AND BORIC ACID.

BY

DR. OSCAR LIEBREICH,

O. Ö. PROFESSOR DER UNIVERSITÄT BERLIN UND GEHEIMER MEDIZINALRAT.

BERLIN, 1902.

58

SUPPLEMENT II.

PREFACE.

IN the Second Treatise on the effects of Borax and Boric Acid, it was still found possible to include in Supplement I. the consideration of the publication in the " Reichsanzeiger " of February 24th, 1902. Later on, reports by the Kaiserliches Gesundheitsamt[1] were published, to review which necessitates a second supplement. Seven treatises had to be considered, besides a great number of tables and curves. This required time, and great accuracy of examination was necessary, especially as a curve of Dr. Rost's [Plate 3, No. 1 (A)] proved at first sight to be incorrectly drawn, and when checking the addition relating to the excretion of Borax, I found some inaccuracy. Moreover, the difficulties of forming a judgment were also increased by the fact that, especially in Dr. Rost's report, contradictions frequently appeared.

All these treatises have only become known since the promulgation of the law in question. Such a proceeding cannot be called a practical one, and it would, perhaps, have been better to have acted in the same way as was done in England. There, 78 experts, among them official authorities, scientific men, naturalists, and distinguished physicians, were examined, and their opinions published,[2] so that a public scientific opinion could be formed. The result of the enquiry in England, moreover, was that the addition of Borax to foods, other than milk, may be allowed within certain limits.

My first investigation into the use of Borax and Boric Acid as a food preservative was made at the instigation of Professor Virchow. The question arose, whether fish caught in deep-sea fishing and preserved with Borax and Boric Acid was injurious to health. I was able, without the further proofs being published—since the innocuousness of the substance was already

---

[1] Vol. 19, No. 1. Numbers of pages appearing in the text without further particulars refer to this publication.

[2] Report of the Departmental Committee appointed to enquire into the Use of Preservatives and Colouring Matters in the Preservation and Colouring of Food, together with Minutes of Evidence, Appendices, and Index. London, 1901.

generally known at that time—to give my opinion that the fish might be eaten without hesitation, and this was acted upon very freely during 8—14 days. Subsequently, representatives of the chemical industry desired me to express an opinion. I undertook to comply with this request—since the question was also of extensive scientific interest—*on condition that any unfavourable data which might be contained in my report should be published equally with the favourable results.* I may further remark that the chemical industry did not require an expert's opinion with the object of trying, under any circumstances, to maintain the right of refining Borax for food preservative purposes, but in order to decide whether the manufacture and sale of Boron compounds might be continued without injury to the consumers.

ASSIMILATION OF FOOD.

With regard to the assimilation of food in the intestines, later experiments have shown that the unfavourable opinions which were formerly held on the subject may be abandoned. They were founded on the experiments of FORSTER, CHITTENDEN, and LIEBREICH. But these views have been considerably modified in favour of Borax. In fact, the conclusion may be drawn from the experiments on metabolism, which have been published in the reports of the Kaiserliches Gesundheitsamt, that the nitrogenous contents of the faeces do not *increase* but rather *decrease* on the administration of Boric Acid. The following curves, giving the nitrogenous contents of the faeces in grammes, illustrate this assertion best.

Contents of Nitrogen in the Fæces.

Metabolism experiment III. Subject S., Page 33.

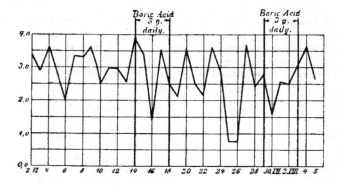

Metabolism experiment IV. Subject W., Page 34.

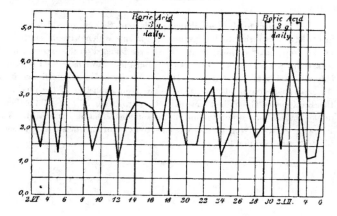

Metabolism experiment V. Subject B., Page 39.

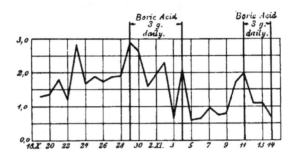

Metabolism experiment VI. Subject A., Page 40.

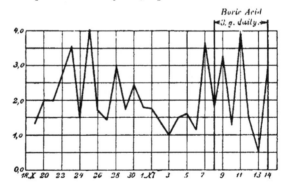

62

A collaborator at the "Reichsgesundheitsamt," R. O. NEUMANN, says himself (p. 95) :—

"With regard to the assimilation of food when taking Borax,
"I was forced to conclude from the present experiment—contrary
"to FORSTER's experiment with Boric Acid—that the assimilation
"was not affected by doses of 3—5 grammes daily."

Only one experiment of HEFFTER's contradicts it.

Nor can the physiological experiments made by Dr. ROST, for judging of the absorption of nitrogen in food containing Boron preparations, be designated as affording any proof. Dr. ROST says on p. 16 :—

"In accordance with the doctrines of the equilibrium of nitrogen,
"the quantity of nitrogen appearing in the urine of one day affords
"a standard for the quantity of albuminous nitrogen absorbed in
"the intestine. Moreover, albumen is, besides carbohydrates,
"one of the food substances which are most speedily assimilated into
"the fluids of the body, so that even during the first hour after
"the consumption of food rich in albumen, the quantity of nitrogen
"in the urine increases, and reaches its maximum within two to
"four (six) hours. Therefore, it must be possible, by means of
"hourly measuring the quantity of nitrogen in the urine passed
"after taking a breakfast of known albuminous contents, as
"compared with the quantity after the administration of Boric
"Acid at breakfast, to ascertain whether Boric Acid has an effect
"within a definite time (three—four hours) on the absorption
"of food-stuffs containing nitrogen."

Dr. ROST thinks that it is possible, by testing the urine for nitrogen, to detect the Boric Acid, so to say, at the moment of its taking effect. His experiments are set out in the two following tables :—[1]

---

[1] The quantity of urine and the excretion of phosphoric acid have been left out as being immaterial for these observations.

Experiment on Dr. S., 27th February to 5th March, 1901.

Commencement of the preparatory experiment, 7.30, breakfast (60 grammes of plasmon, 10 grammes of meat extract, 3 grammes of common salt, 400 ccm. of hot water, 8 grammes of nitrogen) 9.30 to 9.35. End of experiment, 12.30.

Date.	Boric Acid.	TOTAL NITROGEN IN URINE.				
		Before Breakfast.		After Breakfast.		
	grms.	1st Hour. 7.30 to 8.30.	2nd Hour. 8.30 to 9.30.	1st Hour. 9.30 to 10.30.	2nd Hour. 10.30 to 11.30.	3rd Hour. 11.30 to 12.30.
27 Feb.	—	0·644	0·705	0·889	0·908	0·726
28	—	0·718	0·724	0·750	1·021	0·764
1 Mar.	—	0·785	0·749	0·785	0·909	0·784

For making the Plasmon soup, hot water containing 1, 2 and 3 grammes of Boric Acid was used.

2	1	0·777	0·800	**0·855**	**1·047**	**0·879**
3	2	0·898	0·885	**0·963**	**1·039**	**0·969**
4	3	0·798	0·730	**0·769**	**0·546**	**0·885**
5	—	0·692	0·582	0·661	0·837	0·735

Experiment on Dr. Fr., 24th March to 31st March, 1901.

Commencement of the preparatory experiment 6 a.m.; after emptying the bladder, 130 ccm. of Fachinger water. Breakfast (35 grammes of tropon, 80 grammes of tropon biscuits, 3 grammes of tea, 15 grammes of sugar, 350 ccm. of hot water, 8 grammes of nitrogen) 8 to 8.10. This food was eaten with great appetite, probably chiefly on account of the addition of solid

64

food (contrary to Dr. S., who complained of an uncomfortable feeling in the stomach during the experiment, and laid the blame on the absence of solid food). End of the experiment 12.

Date.	Boric acid.	TOTAL NITROGEN IN URINE.					
		Before Breakfast.		After Breakfast.			
	grms.	1st Hour 6 to 7.	2nd Hour 7 to 8.	1st Hour 8 to 9.	2nd Hour 9 to 10.	3rd Hour 10 to 11.	4th Hour 11 to 12.
24 Mar.	—	0·638	0·438	0·686	0·766	0·773	0·752
25	—	0·732	0·650	0·781	0·823	0·888	0·809
26	—	0·784	0·638	0·738	0·864	0·732	0·638

1, 2 and 3 grammes of Boric Acid were added to the hot water used for making the tea and for mixing with the tropon.

27 Mar.	1	0·675	0·631	**0·723**	**0·721**	**0·799**	**0·805**
28	2	0·773	0·735	**0·850**	**0·823**	**0·829**	**0·851**
29	3	0·858	0·700	**0·734**	**0·773**	**0·921**	**0·829**
30	—	0·672	0·582	0 641	0·683	0·770	0·738
31	—	0·739	0·689	0·768	0·703	0·713	0 759

As the result of his experiments, Dr. Rost comes to the following conclusion :—

" A decreasing effect on the assimilation of albuminous food in " the intestine is peculiar to Boron compounds, showing itself with " even small quantities (0·5 gramme). This has been proved by " means of assimilation and metabolism experiments on animals " and human beings, and, moreover, ascertained as occurring in " the first hours after the consumption of Boric Acid by indirect " experiments (viz., observing the curve of the excretion of " nitrogen in the urine and the curve of the temperature after food " containing Boric Acid)."

Such a conclusion is justifiable and of decisive value *only* when there are a number of observations which put the possibility of chance having played a part beyond doubt.

Here only *two* series of experiments are produced. Further, the results of the figures in the two tables by no means coincide. But if we consider the tables as conclusive, they only prove the absorption to be altered in point of time. If in the first table the third hour be included in the calculation, it will be seen that there is no difference at all between the period when food containing Boric Acid was used and that when no Boric Acid was used.

Let us add up the quantity of nitrogen in the urine in the preparatory experiment **before** *breakfast in three days and also the quantity of nitrogen in the urine in the preparatory experiment* **after** *breakfast in the three days, the difference is then* **3·111**. *If we apply the same reckoning to the three days on which Boric Acid was taken, the difference proves to be* **3·055 ;** *it is, therefore, practically the same.* Moreover, it must be remarked that in these experiments, in consequence of the nature of the diet given to the persons in question, an intestinal disturbance took place, which is not wonderful, for a breakfast of 60 grammes of plasmon, 10 grammes of meat extract, 3 grammes of common salt, and 400 ccm. of hot water taken for several days does not agree with everyone. I will not go into further details as to the digestibility of the several substances.

But the correctness of my assertions may be seen even from Dr. Rost's tables. We see that *this injury increases from day to day* ; for in the previous period the difference in the excretion of nitrogen before breakfast and after breakfast is **1·124** on the first day, already less on the second day, namely, **1·093,** on the third day it is **0·894**. Hence, *without Boric Acid being given,* the absorption of nitrogen in the intestine becomes less from day to day. Then Boric Acid is given, and thereupon the excretion of nitrogen suddenly increases, that is, on the first day to **1·204,** decreasing to **1·188** on the second day, and becoming **0·663** on the third day. *This shows quite distinctly that the absorption of nitrogen in the intestine becomes more favourable immediately after the food containing Boric Acid.*

The last figure is not to be wondered at, when we consider that it is the sixth day of Dr. S's. injury to the intestine.

F

The second experiment follows a precisely similar course. On the first day of the preparatory period the difference is **1·149**, the second day it drops to **1·105**, and on the third day to **0·912**. On the fourth day the administration of Borax begins, **thereupon the excretion of nitrogen through the urine increases again, that is, the absorption of nitrogen in the intestine increases;** here the figure is **0·937**, the second day **0·994**, and on the third day, as in the preparatory period, the figures are at their lowest, viz., **0·875**. The differences calculated by me are made clear in the following Table :—

EXPERIMENT I. (Dr. S.)			EXPERIMENT II. (Dr. Fr.)		
Preliminary period :	1st day	... 1·124	Preliminary period : 1st day	... 1·149
	2nd ,,	... 1·098	2nd ,,	... 1·105
	3rd ,,	... 0·894	3rd ,,	... 0·912
Boric Acid period :	4th ,,	... 1·204	Boric Acid period : 4th ,,	... 0·937
	5th ,,	... 1·188	5th ,,	... 0·994
	6th ,,	... 0·668	6th ,,	... 0·875

The after-period should not have been taken into account by Dr. ROST in his observations, as the two persons no longer felt well. After these figures one must at once attribute the injury to the health not to the Boric Acid, but to the most unusual character of the breakfast.

Thus, in opposition to Dr. ROST's conclusions, the following facts may be deduced from his experiments :—

1. Every day of the diet without Boric Acid the conditions of absorption in the intestine become worse in consequence of unsuitable food.

2. According to these experiments, Boric Acid produced a favourable effect on the absorbing capacity of the intestine.

Also Dr. ROST's conclusion on p. 55, viz. :—

> " A decreasing effect on the assimilation of albuminous food in
> " the intestine is peculiar to Boron preparations, showing itself even
> " with small quantities (0·5g.)."

cannot be maintained after the above-mentioned observations, but rather R. O.

NEUMANN'S view must be recognised as correct, **that a diminished assimilation of food does not occur after the addition of Boron preparations.**

ELIMINATION OF BORON PREPARATIONS FROM THE SYSTEM.

A large number of experiments on the elimination of Borax and Boric Acid from the system are in existence. Strangely enough, special importance has been frequently attached to this excretion, which, however, does not apply to these experiments, for it is in itself of no importance whether small quantities of an innocuous matter remain a few days more or less in the system. Dr. ROST says on p. 56, No. 6 :—

> "The complete elimination of Boric Acid from the body takes "place slowly; it may last for days, and, in the case of persons with "kidney disease, for weeks, by which the contingency of accumulation "and a possible cumulative effect is presented."

Firstly, the elimination does *not* take place so slowly, as will be shown in the following experiments; and, secondly, it is quite natural that in kidney diseases the elimination should be retarded, as is also the case with all other substances, even such as are produced by the organism itself. The retardation of the excretion in the case of persons with kidney disease cannot be taken into consideration in judging of the effect of food and substances accompanying the same. I have already given my opinion on the subject in my second treatise on p. 14, in connection with MACNAUGHTON'S experiments on himself. It may first be mentioned here that Borax is one of those substances which completely disappear out of the system—at least, the proof of this fact has been established in the case of animals. Two dogs, weighing 8·64 kg. and 8 kg. were fed on five consecutive days, one with 1·5 grm. of Borax daily, dissolved in 60 ccm. of water, the other dog with 1·5 grm. of Boric Acid dissolved in 60 ccm. of water, which substances were mixed in their usual food. The animals were killed thirty hours after. No more Borax could be found in the organs.

The results in the case of human beings varied considerably. It has been shown that Boric Acid may disappear from the urine on the 5th or 6th day (see p. 15 of my second treatise); in other experiments, Boric reaction has still been found in the urine on the 11th day. But attention must be drawn to the fact that in cases of protracted excretion of Boric Acid in the urine, the food should have been examined as to whether it had not been " borated," or whether food containing Boric Acid in its natural state had not been copiously partaken of. The excretion cannot be a greatly prolonged one, for the cases of the swift disappearance of the Boron preparations from the urine are more convincing than the cases in which, without the above-mentioned precautions, Boric Acid was discovered for a lengthened period. SONNTAG p. 110) submitted to the troublesome examination of the daily excretion of Boric Acid.

In the first experiment, after taking 3 grammes of Boric Acid, in 77 hours 2·679 grammes, i.e., 89·30 °/₀, were recovered. In the case of another person experimented on, 2·931 grammes, i e., 97·7 °/₀, were found in 96 hours.

In the third series of experiments, after taking 3 grammes, in 108 hours 3·048 grammes were found, *that is, more than was administered*, expressed as a percentage, viz., 101·59 °/₀, *the excretion still continuing*. This remarkable result was not noticed by SONNTAG, but had to be checked, as in this series of experiments the percentage at the end is not given as in the first two cases. The result is easily explained, as the determination of Boric Acid in such small quantities is liable to error. No blame is due to Mr. SONNTAG on account of the analytical mistake, but it is certainly a great fault of editorship to create a false impression, through inexact statements, on the reader, who is not capable of calculating these things so quickly. It is not the reader's business to calculate, but the experimenter's business to produce the calculation worked out.

The entire experiments are, moreover, so useless for judging of the question, for the reason that the small quantities of Boric Acid remaining in the system are of no importance. *Even should an accumulation take place* these quantities could not cause poisoning. During the administration of Boric Acid to human beings, continued for months, so-called symptoms of accumulation must have appeared; they have, however, never been observed, nor have they ever been noticed in experiments on animals.

Thus the conclusion quoted above, drawn by Dr. ROST from these experiments, is entirely unfounded, and the following fact must be stated :—**Boron preparations remain by no means remarkably long in the system, but are excreted from the system normally like most other substances.** A detention in the system may naturally occur if *the* *kidneys are impassable*, and this symptom occurs *in the case of all other substances* which are taken, and likewise substances produced by the organism itself. **But even in the case of persons with diseased kidneys, the detention of Boric Acid in the system can lead to no further injury of the health.**

DIARRHŒA.

Alleged Diarrhœtic Effect of Borax and Boric Acid.

Dr. Rost says, on p. 55: "Yet in not too small quantities they (the "Boron preparations) produce diarrhœa," and on p. 57: "The possibility of "causing a *diarrhœtic condition* . . . . . . forces us to class Boron "preparations with the pharmacologically injurious substances"

There are no proofs of this.

It is true that in Kister's experiments on three persons, one person got diarrhœa after taking 3 grammes. This appearance in the case of one person, as opposed to two persons who did not get diarrhœa, cannot be cited as a proof.

Then Dr. Rost refers to Mitscherlich's experiments on rabbits in which overdoses of 1·9 grammes and in another case of 3·75 grammes were used. Among the symptoms which appeared, Rost also mentions "symptoms of colicky pains." It is by no means evident how colicky pains can be observed in rabbits: in all my long experience I have not succeeded in making such an observation.

Further, when Heffter (p. 98) states that Mattern, in his experiment on himself, observed slight diarrhœa after taking 2 grammes of Borax in a 4 °/₀ solution, this case must be entirely rejected as evidence, for it is not a question of whether a salt agrees with one *in an aqueous solution*, but of whether it does so when mixed with food. If 2 grammes of common salt in a 4 °/₀ solution be drunk, it only depends on whether the stomach contains a large quantity of food or not whether in this case pains in the stomach and slight diarrhœa will not also occur.

Heffter also cites Le Bon (p. 98) as proof, and says that even small quantities of Borax added to meat cause unpleasant symptoms in the intestine and *even diarrhœa*. This statement, however, is no to be found in Le Bon. I repeat Le Bon's words here :—

"Plongée quelques heures dans une solution de borax pur ou "simplement entourée de borax en poudre, la viande se conserve "sans altération pendant un temps fort long ; mais lorsqu'on "l'emploie comme aliment après quelques semaines, cette viande "produit des troubles intestinaux qui ont obligé à renoncer à son "emploi. Le borax, pris à petites doses répétées, est une substance "toxique dont l'usage dans la conservation des substances alimentaires "me paraît devoir être sévèrement proscrit." (Compt. rend. 1878, p. 936.)

One sees that Le Bon made his observations on badly preserved meat and the conclusion he draws, that Borax in small doses is a poisonous substance, is consequently unfounded. The injuries he claims to have observed—although only in a single case—were evidently caused by products of decomposition. *But diarrhœa is not so much as hinted at.* Le Bon only speaks of "troubles intestinaux." Whereas Heffter quotes "unpleasant symptoms in the intestine and even diarrhœa." This latter symptom is Heffter's own arbitrary addition ; for "troubles intestinaux" may be colicky pains and anything else, but Le Bon *did not report diarrhœa.*

Dr. Rost, as already mentioned above, makes the following statement (p. 55) :—"Yet in not too small quantities they produce diarrhœa" ; and further on, "Besides causing diarrhœa, the possibility of irritation of the "intestine, leading to disintegration of cells and increased secretion of mucus, "must be admitted to be the cause of protraction and deterioration in the "function of absorption."

In this paragraph the effect after not too small doses of producing diarrhœa is first mentioned, and at its conclusion one can see that this effect is accepted as an established fact. We must, therefore, investigate the views by means of which Dr. Rost has arrived at this false conclusion. He says, on p. 10 :—

"If Boric Acid or Borax be taken in food, any *local* effects "thereof will be felt on the coating of the stomach and intestine. "This may appear in various subjective complaints, such as, at the

71

"*post-mortem* examination (in experiments on animals), signs of red-
"ness, inflammation or slight corrosion of the stomach and intestinal
"canal, or in increased secretion of digestive fluid and increased
"intestinal peristaltic action, recognisable by the formation and
"composition of the fæces (diarrhœa)."

Dr. Rost refers to experiments on animals to prove this. But these are
not pertinent.

Two series of experiments have been made :—

Firstly, Boric Acid or Borax were communicated to the animals *subcutaneously*; and, secondly, *through the stomach*. The first series of these
experiments cannot be used to form any conclusions; it is well known that it
is not permissible to examine *subcutaneously* substances *which are never given
subcutaneously* to human beings for the definite purpose of serving as food.
This need not be discussed in detail, for it is known that digested albuminoid
substances, peptones, have, when injected, a poisonous effect, whereas they are
daily sent out by the stomach and absorbed for purposes of nutrition. If we
wished, for instance, to test the utility of meat extract, it would not do to try
it by means of subcutaneous injections, for it is known that a dose which,
when administered through the stomach, agrees with an animal perfectly well,
injures the animal extremely when subcutaneously administered. Many
similar examples might easily be produced, so that no further proof is
necessary that *experiments conducted subcutaneously* can give no profitable
result, the more so that it has never been denied that in the case of human
beings injurious effects may occur when Borax and Boric Acid are injected
into cavities of the body in immoderate quantities. Nevertheless, as the
subcutaneous experiments are intended also to be made use of for other
conclusions, the experiments made shall be submitted to criticism. The
following table gives a summary of the experiments made by Dr. Rost.

Subcutaneous Experiments with Borax and Boric Acid on Rabbits.

Experiment.	Weight of Rabbits. grammes.	—	Dose.	Water. ccm.
1	2450	Boric Acid	2·4	80
2	3100	Borax	5·7*	100
3	2250	,,	3 8*	80
4	2220	,,	1·9*	50
12	2000	Boric Acid	2	100
			2	100
13	2200	Borax	4·7*	50
25	1900	,,	9·6* (In 18 days)	380
63	1200	Boric Acid	1·2	40
64	1195	Borax	2 3*	40

*These doses marked with an asterisk are calculated to correspond to ordinary Borax containing water of crystallization ; the author has not worked out the figures uniformly, as is necessary for comparison, but he gives partly Borax containing water, partly anhydrous Borax.

It may be seen from the doses that it is in almost all cases a question of 1 gramme or more per kilogramme. These doses are in themselves very large ; further, 50-100 · ccm. of *water are injected under the animal's skin.* This *inundation* with the substance to be examined can lead to no decisive result, and all comparisons drawn by Dr. Rost with soda, hydrochloric acid and other matters, are not pertinent, because the local effect and the rapidity of absorption cannot be compared.

It may be here remarked that even in these experiments, as experiment No. 3 shows, with 3·8 grammes of Borax in 80 ccm. of water, *no diarrhœa* was found, nor in the fourth experiment with 1·9 grammes of Borax in 50 ccm. of water. Likewise experiment No. 25 is of no use for forming an opinion on the "chronic supply of Borax," as in this case also the administration was subcutaneous

Naturally, the animals die in the end under these experiments, and this is accompanied by the most varied symptoms. The discussion of the length of time and manner in which the animals died admits of no conclusion being drawn as to the poisonous effect of Boric Acid, but on the contrary leads to the opinion that Boric Acid must be considered harmless, since such large doses and such an immoderate supply of water were necessary to kill the animals.

If we now turn to the experiments through the stomach, Dr. ROST's experiments may be seen from the following table :—

Experiments with Borax and Boric Acid on Rabbits through the Stomach.

Experiment.	Weight of Rabbits grammes.	—	Dose. grammes.	Water. ccm.	—
18	2300	Boric Acid.	3	100	
			3	100	
19	2200	,,	1·5	50	
			1·5	50	
			1·5	50	
			1·5	50	
			1·5	50	
			1·5	50	
20	2650	,,	7·5	250	Within 4¼ hours
26	1250	,,	14·0	400	Within 4¼ hours
30	1170	,,	5·5	110	
		Borax	0·5	10	8½ hour later injected into the vein
		Borax	0·5	10	6 minutes later
57	1620	Boric Acid Borax	12·0} 7·0}	100	
62	1425	Borax Boric Acid	7·0} 10·0}	100	

Firstly, it is seen that the rabbit's stomach was overburdened with too great a quantity. Doses of 3 grammes to 14 grammes of Boric Acid were applied ; further, a mixture of Boric Acid and Borax, and that in the enormous quantity of 19 (!) and 17 (!) grammes.

The abnormal method in which these experiments were conducted, by the way, may be seen from the following facts :—

A rabbit weighing 2,300 grammes (experiment No. 18) received twice a day 3 grammes of Boric Acid and 200 ccm. of water besides. The second animal (experiment No. 19) received 1·5 grammes of Boric Acid in 50 ccm. of water six times from 6th to 12th February, 1901. In the first experiment diarrhœa occurred. As in the second experiment, soft fæcal balls and at midday slight diarrhœa appeared only on February 12th after the last dose of Boric Acid, the experimenter seems to have lost patience, and in order to establish the diarrhœa he wished for, he gave the rabbit, *which had previously been left without food for* 24 *hours,* 7·5 grammes in 250 ccm. of water within 4¼ hours (experiment 20). Thereupon profuse diarrhœa was produced. But even the result of this severe experiment is nullified by experiment No. 57. The experimenter here gave 12 (!) grammes of Boric Acid and 7 (!) grammes of Borax in 100 ccm. of water! This animal showed no diarrhœa; consequently another experiment of this kind with 7 grammes of Borax and 10 grammes of Boric Acid was made, which finally produced diarrhœa. In another experiment (26), 14 grammes of Boric Acid in 400 ccm of water were administered to a small rabbit weighing only 1,250 grammes within 4¼ hours. The mere introduction of such large quantities of water with the Boron preparations means an injury.

Since a rabbit's stomach, even fasting, still contains a considerable quantity of remains of food, an inflation must have taken place. Here, therefore, a new phase appears, namely, the inflation of the stomach with the simultaneous action of a drug, an effect which has not yet been scientifically investigated, since it was of no interest in any way. But we are not acquainted with the result of inundating the stomach of an animal with water and drugs. But especially should the temperature have been taken into account, for it makes a difference whether the animal's stomach be inflated with cold or warm water. In the case of human beings, 18 litres of water poured into the stomach in the water-torture, which was considered a mild torture, are said not to have proved fatal, but they survived it only on condition that they were *subsequently thoroughly warmed.* The experience we possess on this subject is taken from descriptions of the water-torture in the Middle Ages.

> "Celui qui devait la subir était, comme pour la question
> "précédente, attaché et soutenu en l'air par les quatre membres,
> "jusqu'à ce que son corps fût bien étendu. On lui passait alors un
> "tréteau sous les reins, et à l'aide d'une corne formant entonnoir,
> "pendant qu'on lui serrait le nez avec la main pour le contraindre
> "d'avaler, on lui versait lentement dans la bouche quatre coquemars.

75

"d'eau (environ neuf litres) pour la question ordinaire, et le double
"pour la question extraordinaire. L'exécution terminée, le patient
"était détaché 'et mené chauffer dans la cuisine,' dit un vieux
"texte." [1]

αₓₚₐ *Therefore the effect of Boron preparations of producing diarrhœa cannot be
deduced from the second group of experiments either.*

*Even such large doses as these, which do not come into question for use in
food, produce no diarrhœa in human beings.* This is best proved by the statements found in Dr. Rost's treatise (see p. 11). Binswanger perceived no
diarrhœa after 3·75 grammes of Borax divided into four doses—I will not go
into the other symptoms as it is here only a question of diarrhœa—nor
any complaints after 1½ drachms of Boric Acid. Boric Acid taken in the
morning at 8 and 9 o'clock in doses of 1 drachm each time (total 7½ grammes)
caused no inconvenience at all, and even after Binswanger had taken 3·75
grammes of Boric Acid again at 9.45, no diarrhœa occurred. As Dr. Rost states,
Polli, Wildner, Johnson, Vigier, and Rosenthal found much the same.
We read "larger doses (4—6 grammes) produced considerable nausea and
thirst, 10—15 grammes vomiting, loss of appetite and severe diuresis." Yet
nothing is said of diarrhœa. I may repeat, moreover, that these symptoms
may also occur after the same doses of chloride of sodium. Dr. Rost himself
observed no diarrhœa after 3 grammes of Boric Acid in a cup of coffee. Let
us trace the cases further. Dr. Sonntag, author of one of the treatises of the
"Reichsgesundheitsamt " took altogether six grammes of Boric Acid on the
2nd, 3rd, and 4th March (p. 17); he interrupted the experiment, because
among other symptoms, *constipation* had set in. The person experimented on.
Dr. Fritzweiler, took in all six grammes on the 27th, 28th, and 29th March
(p. 18), and noticed pain in the stomach, but no diarrhœa. Besides, the
absence of good health is not remarkable in itself from a medical point of
view, considering the diet, namely, 35 grammes of tropon, 80 grammes
of tropon biscuits, 3 grammes of tea, 15 grammes of sugar, and 350 ccm.
of hot water continued for a week. At all events, diarrhœa did not occur.

Subject **A.** (p. 29) took 3 grammes of Boric Acid daily from November
21st to December 2nd, that is for twelve days, without having diarrhœa. The
quantity of fæces in the previous period was, on an average, 139 grammes,

---

[1] Mœurs, Usages et Coutumes au Moyen Age et à l'Epoque de la Renaissance, par Paul
Lacroix. p. 439. Paris 1874.

containing 74·2 °/₀ of water ; during the period of twelve days in which Boric Acid was taken, it was 101 grammes, containing 72·7 °/₀ of water, and in the after-period 105 grammes, containing 75·9 °/₀ of water. This forms the following table :—

Days.	Boric Acid. grammes.	Fæces. grammes.	Water. grammes.	Water. per cent.
7	0	139	108·6	74·3
12	36	101	94·9	72·7
5	0	105	80·0	75·9

Subject B. (p. 30) took 3 grammes of Boric Acid daily for 12 days, without having diarrhœa. In the five previous days the quantity of the fæces was 52·4 grammes, containing 64·7 °/₀ water ; during the twelve days in which Boric Acid was taken, 56·9 grammes, containing 67·8 °/₀ water ; in the subsequent five days, 65·9 grammes, containing 64·3 °/₀ water. The following table results :—

Days.	Boric Acid. grammes.	Fæces. grammes.	Water. grammes.	Water. per cent.
5	0	52·4	33·9	64·7
12	36	56·9	38·6	67·8
5	0	65·9	42·4	64·3

In the case of subject S. (p. 33) the following interesting discovery was made : the individual had had a total of 46 stools from the 2nd to the 13th June, of these on two days five times each, on five days four times each, on three days three times each, and on one day once, that is, on an average, **3·83** stools. While taking Boric Acid from June 14th to June 18th in quantities of 3 grammes daily, only 9 stools were evacuated in five days, and none at all on two days, that is on an average only **1·8** stools. In the subsequent period of ten days, during which, of course, there was still Boric Acid in the system, only nine evacuations of the bowels occurred, that is on an average **0·9.**

77

There then followed a period of five days with 3 grammes of Boric Acid daily, but added to that 50 grammes of bacon. Notwithstanding, the number of stools was only nine, on one day none, and on an average **1·8**. The following period of two days shows two stools daily. In the previous period of twelve days, the average of the quantity of fæces was 436 grammes, containing 87·4 °/₀ of water, in the Boric Acid period of five days, 332 grammes, containing 87·9 °/₀ of water, in the subsequent period of ten days, 212 grammes, containing 83·7 °/₀ of water. In the following period of five days, in which Boric Acid was given in quantities of 3 grammes and bacon of 50 grammes daily, the quantity of fæces was 222 grammes, containing 84·2 °/₀ of water, in the subsequent period of two days without Boric Acid, 395 grammes containing 88·8 °/₀ of water.

This gives the following enlarged Table :—

Days.	Boric Acid.	Fæces. grammes.	Water. grammes.	Water. per cent.	Number of Stools.	Average Number of Stools.
12	0	436	381	87·4	46	3·83
5	15	332	292	87·8	9	1·8
10	0	212	177·5	83·7	9	0·9
5	15	222	187	84·2	9	1·8
2	0	395	351	88·8	4	2

In the case of subject W. (p. 34), 19 stools were evacuated from the 2nd to the 13th June, on three days none : on an average 1·58. In the following five days from June 14th to June 18th, while taking 3 grammes of Boric Acid daily, six stools occurred, two days were without stools : on an average 1·2 stools. Again in the after-period, in which there was still Boric Acid in the patient's body, nine stools were discharged from June 19th to June 28th— that is in ten days—no stools on six days, making on an average 0·9 stool. On the following five days from June 29th to July 3rd, in which 3 grammes of Boric Acid were given and 50 grammes of bacon were added, *no stool occurred at all* on the first days, two stools on July 2nd, three on July 7th : equals an average of one stool daily. In the subsequent period of three days, six took place, that is two stools daily. With regard to the amount of the fæces, it

78

was as follows: In the twelve days of the previous period, 153 grammes of fæces, containing 79·7 % of water, were evacuated ; on the following five days, when Boric Acid was given in doses of 3 grammes each, the amount of fæces was 151 grammes, with 77·5 % of water ; on the ten succeeding days, in which no Boric Acid was given, an increase of the amount of the fæces to 182 grammes, containing 80·8 % of water, took place ; on the five following days, with 3 grammes of Boric Acid each, the weight of the fæces sinks to 178 grammes, with the small amount of moisture of 79·2 % ; in the next three days, without Boric Acid, 121 grammes of fæces, with 81 % of water, is evacuated.

This gives the following Table :—

Days.	Boric Acid.	Fæces. grammes.	Water. grammes.	Water. per cent.	Number of Stools.	Average Number of Stools.
12	0	153	122	79·7	19	1·58
5	15	151	117	77·5	6	1·2
10	0	182	147	80·8	9	0·9
5	15	178	141	79·2	5	1
3	0	121	98	81	6	2

In the case of the last two persons experimented on, the number of whose stools is also stated, we also see *rather a retardation* than an increase of the fæcal evacuations.

As for subject A., VI. (p. 40), in the preliminary period of seven days the amount of the fæces is 165 grammes, containing 78·8 % water. After 350 ccm. less liquid has been given, the amount of the fæces in ten days proves to be 93 grammes per day, containing 73·1 % water. In the respiratory chamber the amount of the fæces in three days is on an average 101 grammes, containing 72·2 % water. Then follows the Boric Acid period in the respiratory chamber, lasting five days with 3 grammes of Boric Acid daily : the amount of the fæces is 158 grammes, with 81 % of water ; outside the chamber with 3 grammes of Boric Acid the amount of the fæces is 94 grammes, with 74·5 % of water.

This gives the following Table :—

Days.	Boric Acid. grammes.	Fæces. grammes.	Water. grammes.	Water. per cent.
7	6	165	130	78 8
10	0	98*	68	73 1
3	0	101	73	72·2
5	15	158	128	81
2	6	94	70	74 5

* 350 ccm. less fluid (beer) was drunk.

Subject B., V. (p. 39), who also received 3 grammes of Boric Acid every day for five days, and then again on two days, had no diarrhœa either In the previous period of seven days the average weight of the fæces was 79·3 grammes, containing 69·9 % water ; during the preceding period of three days in the respiratory chamber, 77·7 grammes, containing 68·2 % water ; weight of fæces during the Boric Acid period of five days in the respiratory chamber, with 3 grammes of Boric Acid a day, 111·2 grammes, containing 74·5 % water ; outside the apparatus on two days, with 3 grammes of Boric Acid, 56·5 grammes, with 67·3 % of water ; in the subsequent period of 6 days, without Boric Acid, fæces 37·2 grammes, with 61·9 % water, and finally in the following period of four days, with 3 grammes of Boric Acid a day, 52 grammes of fæces, containing 63·5 % water.

This gives the following Table :—

Days.	Boric Acid. grammes.	Fæces. grammes.	Water. grammes.	Water. per cent.
7	0	79·3	55	69·9
3	0	77·7	53	68·2
5	15	111·2	82·8	71·5
2	6	56·5	38	67·3
6	0	37·2*	23	61·9
4	12	52	33	63·5

* In Dr. ROST'S treatise the figure is wrongly given as 42.

80

I may still mention here the experiment in the report of the "Kaiserliches Gesundheitsamt" made by Dr. R. O. NEUMANN, viz., the experiment on metabolism with Borax. He says, on p. 93 :—

> "Before and after the experiment, as well as during the same, "I was in perfect health. It was completed without interruption, "and without special trouble."

The following interesting figures result from his experiment on metabolism :—In the preliminary period, 260 grammes of fæces with 231·5 grammes of water, *i.e.*, a percentage of 89·0. Thereupon, Dr. R. O. NEUMANN takes 3 grammes of Borax daily for ten days ; during this time the weight of the fæces sinks to 212 grammes, containing 90% of water. In the intervening period of four days without Borax, the quantity of the fæces increases to 236 grammes, containing 82·8%, of water. In the subsequent period of three days in which Borax in the augmented dose of 5 grammes daily was taken, the amount of the fæces sinks to 198 grammes, containing 83·5 % of water.

It gives the following Table :—

Days.	Borax.	Fæces. grammes.	Water. grammes.	Water. per cent.
4	0	260	231	89
10	30	212	190·9	90
4	0	236	195·4	82·8
3	15	198	165·5	83·5

Likewise in the case of the patients treated by me no diarrhœa occurred, although very large doses were made use of. The figures will be given here :—

In 24 days ... . 39·9 grammes of Boric Acid.
„ 22 „ ... ... 37·5 „ „
„ 11 „ ... ... 33 „ „
„ 7 „ ... ... 28 „ „
„ 26 „ ... ... 14·1 „ Borax.
„ 32 „ ... ... 88·7 „ „
„ 37 „ ... ... 60·9 „ „
„ 14 „ ... ... 24 „ „
„ 14 „ ... ... 23 „ „

81

Similarly, in the cases reported by GERHARDT, in which the first patient underwent a treatment with Borax lasting 34 days of daily doses varying between 1·5 and 3 grammes, no diarrhœa was observed ; on the contrary, after leaving off Carlsbad salts, a *decrease in the stools* took place to one per day. Also in the case of the second and third patients, who were dangerously ill, no diarrhœa occurred after a prolonged application.[1]

It is interesting to trace the observations made on the application of Boric Acid in cases of tuberculosis. GAUCHER states[2] :—" Il n'a jamais " produit aucun trouble gastro-intestinal. Je dirais même qu'il m'a semblé " *prévenir la diarrhée des phthisiques.*"

Thus, instead of producing diarrhœa, we find after examining medical literature that in some cases the application of Boron preparations has even *decreased the number of stools, and constipation has occurred.*

It will be seen from the following remarks of Dr. ROST, how important a question it is whether Boron preparations may be considered diarrhœtica or not :—

" Also in the provisioning of expeditions and of soldiers in time " of war, when irritation and affections of the intestines occur " frequently, it has rightly been designated a question of the highest " hygienic importance whether preservatives ought to be permitted " or not " (p. 2).

After the above explanations, Borax-preserved foods can safely be used for provisioning expeditions and soldiers on the march, without conscientious scruples of their possibly causing diarrhœa, especially as in practice no such bad effects have ever occurred.

For even such large doses as are quite out of the question for preserving are not capable of producing diarrhœa, as has just been proved. I will over-look the various contradictions, in which Dr. ROST has got entangled, as the only thing of importance is to give really logical evidence. This evidence has shown **that Borax and Boric Acid, even in very large doses, used in food, produce no diarrhœa, and that the opinion cannot be maintained that Borax and Boric Acid belong to the pharma-cologically injurious substances.**

---

[1] Ther. d. Gegenwart. 1902, June.

[2] Le Bulletin Médical, No. 64. 10 Août, 1890, p. 752.

G

82

VOMITING.

In order to prove that Boron preparations produce vomiting, Dr. Rost makes use of the following argument (p. 13):—

> "Thus we see that a dog of 17 kilogrammes vomited repeatedly
> "after 6 grammes of Boric Acid, after so long a time as about
> "twelve hours after taking food; another weighing 10 kilogrammes
> "vomited its usual food once after the addition of only 2 grammes,
> "and a second time after doses gradually increasing up to 5 grammes
> "of Boric Acid, while, under the same conditions,

> "   9 grammes of Borax   (containing water of crystallisation)
> "14   ,,   Soda   ,,   ,,   ,,
> "11   ,,   Saltpetre   ,,   ,,   ,,
> " 0·5 ,,   Fluoride of Sodium   ,,   ,,   ,,
> " 2·0 ,,   Salicylic Acid   ,,   ,,   ,,
> " 0·4 ,,   Formaldehyde   ,,   ,,   ,,
> "25   ,,   Common Salt   ,,   ,,   ,,
> "were either no longer borne, or the food was refused."

Such enormous quantities of irritating and corrosive matters had been given here that we do not find it astonishing that the dog should after this be unable to bear 2 grammes of Borax more and that it should vomit. At all events, these experiments justify no conclusions in the food question.

Another experiment referred to in connection with vomiting must be rejected as utterly unsuitable. This is the "*experiment on a dog fasting*," described on p. 58 in the appendix. The dog, probably the one mentioned above, *was starved for 4 days* (!) and given only 100 ccm. of water per day. On the 5th day after it had lost 750 grammes of its weight, it received 1 gramme of Boric Acid and vomited half an hour after. The next day, the dog having still been kept starving, and *having lost 960 grammes* (!) received 2 grammes of Boric Acid dissolved in 100 ccm. of water and vomited directly after receiving it. The table of this experiment of Dr. Rost's may be given here [1]:—

---

[1] The column giving the secretion of urine has been left out as being irrelevant.

83

Experiment on a Starving Dog.

Every day at a certain time 100 ccm. of water were introduced into the animal's stomach :—

Date.	Bodyweight.	Introduced in 100 ccm. of water, grammes.	Remarks.
7 Mar.	10000	—	
8	9850	—	
9	9650	—	
10	9450	—	
11	9250	1·0	Boric Acid, vomiting after about half-an-hour.
12	9040	2·0	Vomiting directly after introduction of the 2 per cent. solution of Boric Acid.
13	8970	—	
14	8850	—	

It is scarcely comprehensible that such an experiment could be made, for there is in itself nothing remarkable in the fact that an animal should vomit after receiving into its stomach a solution containing Borax on the fifth day of fasting. We know that in the case of human beings and dogs everything except water, even *food*, must be administered with the greatest care after a condition of fasting for some days, as otherwise *vomiting occurs immediately*. It was entirely unnecessary to make such an experiment.

When Dr. Rost refers to one of my feeding experiments as a proof of an emetic effect, this cannot be pertinent, as his demonstration is founded on an incorrect quotation, as has already been stated on p. 46 of the first supplement to my second treatise.

That human beings may occasionally vomit after doses of 4 grammes and more has already been minutely discussed in my first treatise, but this only occurs when the doses are taken on an empty stomach and in an aqueous solution.

Dr. Rost now deducts the following facts from his "experiments" :—

"According to the results of these experiments, and from "observations on human beings, described in the experiments on

G 2

"metabolism, the practical importance attached in many quarters [?]
"to this undoubtedly existing irritation of the stomach, is not
"justified; it can only play a part in large doses of considerable
"concentration and in the case of persons with diseased mucous
"membrane of the stomach."

The conclusion must, however, according to all present experiences, be
formulated as follows :—

**According to the result of Dr. ROST'S experiments
and observations on human beings, Boron preparations
are not emetics. The emetic and irritating action on
the stomach only occurs after considerably larger
doses than come into question in the preservation of
food. It only occurs in human beings after large doses
of considerable concentration. But this latter effect is
of no practical importance as regards the question of
food preserving.**

LOSS OF WEIGHT.

The declaration of the Bundesrat (Federal Council) forbidding the
admixture of Boron preparations to meat, appeared on February 18th, 1902.
On February 24th, there appeared in the "Deutscher Reichsanzeiger":
"the subject-matter, on the strength of which the Bundesrat, in accordance
"with par. 21 of the law relating to the Official Inspection of Meat,
"had drawn up the decree made public in the Chancellor's declaration of
"February, 18th, 1902 (Reichsgesetzbl. p. 48), on injurious and deceptive
"compounds in meat, and preparations thereof."

In the publication of February, 24th, 1902 ("Deutscher Reichsanzeiger u. Königlich Preussischer Staatsanzeiger No. 47, Beilage"), there is a
reference made to the loss of weight supposed to occur after taking food
containing Boron substances.

The only scientific statement about this which had existed until then was
published in the "Hygienische Rundschau" (Hygienic Review), which had
appeared only nine days before, and which became known to the subscribers
about a week later—that is at about the same time as the publication of the
"Reichsanzeiger." The detailed account then appeared later in No. 1 of

Vol. 19 of the "Arbeiten aus dem Kaiserlichen Gesundheitsamt." One might have expected that when a statute was founded on a scientific work, this scientific work would at least be submitted to discussion, and especially would be confirmed in other quarters. The results found by RUBNER were carried out on two persons experimented on, who were in the respiratory chamber, and after leaving the chamber showed a more or less considerable loss of weight. The loss of weight RUBNER attributes, according to his experiments, to the increased waste of fat in consequence of the consumption of Boric Acid. This observation refers to persons who had undergone a considerable fattening treatment and had done no work in the respiratory chamber, whereas they did work after leaving the chamber. The experiments are so very unconvincing, because in the case of person "A" (see Plate III., VI., A) the loss of weight is quite exceptional and does not correspond to the change in weight of the person "B" (see Plate III., V., B), for in this experiment the original weight, before the application of Borax, is much the same as in the subsequent period in which he takes Boric Acid; in fact, at the end of the Borax period, slightly more than the original weight, namely, at the beginning 58·150 grammes and at the end 58·450 grammes.

Moreover, to this is added that subject "A" did not suffer from a similar loss of weight in an experiment with Boric Acid made about a year before (see Plate III., Experiment on Metabolism I., A). In the former experiment, in fact, the weight increased again during the Boric Acid period, which certainly, in consequence of Dr. ROST's incorrectly drawn curve, is not clearly shewn. The impression becomes much clearer when Dr. ROST's curve is corrected; the fault is not considerable, but all the same it gives a wrong idea.

Besides, it must be borne in mind that these experiments were made with such a large dose, namely 3 grammes, as need not come into use in food. Such a proportion has only exceptionally been taken in food, and can be avoided by proper legal regulation.

In another case, a loss of weight was observed later by R. O. NEUMANN. But if we consider NEUMANN's tables in the report of the "Kaiserliches Gesundheitsamt" (p. 93), we first see that the experiments with Borax were begun in a period of decreasing weight; moreover, that the loss of weight after taking 3 grammes of Borax daily for seven days only amounted to 1 kilogramme, and that during this period of seven days the weight began to

86

increase again, so that this case cannot, as NEUMANN wishes, be cited as a proof of loss of weight.

Further, some experiments of C. GERHARDT's[1] have been published. In the case of three patients, who were undergoing treatment for obesity, he simultaneously applied Borax. He says :—

> " Still, it may be said that, according to these few experiments,
> " the dose of 0·25 gramme three times a day has little or no effect,
> " 0·5 gramme acts and agrees well, while 1 gramme (that is 3
> " grammes a day) already produces unfavourable effects."

Here it must be borne in mind that the unfavourable effects were observed in the case of a patient dangerously ill, whose symptoms not having been observed after Borax in other cases, cannot be attributed solely to the latter.

No conclusion can be drawn from these isolated observations, as compared with practical experience, in order to justify the rejection of the use of Boron preparations as preservatives.

Dr. ROST's experiments on loss of weight need not be entered into here, since even RUBNER did not observe such losses of weight in his method of procedure.

KIDNEYS.

In the case of the kidneys, as Dr. ROST also acknowledges, a renewed and close investigation was necessary. Such a one has been reported in my treatise. It shows that no influence on the kidneys can be exercised by Boron compounds. Dr. ROST's reference to the possible influence on the kidneys shows that the whole question of alimentary albuminuria has escaped him, and after my second treatise there is not the faintest possibility of an effect on the kidneys. This, Dr. ROST, it is true, calls in question in some places, whilst in others again he emphasizes it, thus contradicting himself. He says, in fact, on p. 56, No. 8 :—"The existence of a so-called *nephritis borica* has not been " proved until now." But on p. 57, in contradiction to this, he says :—

---

[1] Therapie der Gegenwart, June. 1902.

"We are forced to class Boron preparations with the pharmacologically
"injurious substances, and we are compelled to do so owing to their action
"on the kidneys (excretion of albumen in the urine)." This has been
sufficiently refuted in my second treatise, and consequently this conclusion of
Dr. Rost's falls entirely to the ground. **It is proved, on the contrary,
that Boracic preparations have no injurious effect on the
kidneys.**

CAUSE OF DEATH.

That cases of death may occur through injections of Boron preparations into the cavities of the body and through application to wounds, has
already been mentioned in my first treatise on pp. 4 and 5, and I pointed out
that these cases of death, especially after overdoses, have nothing to do with
the food question. In my first treatise it was mentioned that Boric Acid up
to 25 grammes did no harm. HEFFTER now refers to a case of SCHWYZER'S[1],
in which a man of 60 years and suffering *from severe heart disease*, swallowed
15 grammes of Boric Acid—whether intentionally or by mistake is not clear—
death resulting. The *post-mortem* result is not even given. It is not worth
criticising such an event in a man suffering from acute heart disease ; one can
only say, care should be taken that a man of 60 with heart disease does not
swallow 15 grammes of Boric Acid.

A second case concerns a man of 65, who suffered from *bronchitis and
softening of the brain*, and who had a carbuncle opened on the nape of the neck ;
the wound was covered with powdered Boric Acid. On the fourth day a
cutaneous eruption, a slight *eczema erythematodes*, as is said in the report,
was visible, then loss of appetite, bilious vomiting, and diarrhœa. These
symptoms appear not unusually during the fatal progress of carbuncles, and
in this case it is the less to be wondered at, the man being 65 and suffering
from bronchitis and softening of the brain ! Therefore, it is quite arbitrary
to attribute the cause of death to Boric Acid. But this case must further be
rejected as evidence in the food question, since it is an instance of external
application. Therefore the universal experience that **the internal application of Borax and Boric Acid has never yet proved fatal,**
is not shaken by HEFFTER's statements.

---

[1] " New York Med. Journal," VIII., 263, 1895.

CPSIA information can be obtained
at www.ICGtesting.com
Printed in the USA
LVHW080500050521
686549LV00006B/482